CAMPAIGN 363

# LEUCTRA 371 BC

The Destruction of Spartan Dominance

**MURRAY DAHM**

ILLUSTRATED BY SEÁN Ó'BRÓGÁIN
*Series editor Nikolai Bogdanovic*

OSPREY PUBLISHING
Bloomsbury Publishing Plc
PO Box 883, Oxford, OX1 9PL, UK
29 Earlsfort Terrace, Dublin 2, Ireland
1385 Broadway, 5th Floor, New York, NY 10018, USA
E-mail: info@ospreypublishing.com
**www.ospreypublishing.com**

OSPREY is a trademark of Osprey Publishing Ltd

First published in Great Britain in 2021

© Osprey Publishing Ltd, 2021

A catalogue record for this book is available from the British Library.

ISBN: PB 9781472843517; eBook 9781472843487; ePDF 9781472843494;
XML 9781472843500

21 22 23 24 25    10 9 8 7 6 5 4 3 2 1

Maps by Bounford.com
3D BEVs by Paul Kime
Index by Fionbar Lyons
Typeset by PDQ Digital Media Solutions, Bungay, UK
Printed and bound in India by Replika Press Private Ltd.

MIX
Paper from
responsible sources
FSC® C016779

## Artist's note

Readers may care to note that the original paintings from which the colour
plates in this book were prepared are available for private sale. All
reproduction copyright whatsoever is retained by the publishers. All
enquiries should be addressed to:

seanobrogain@yahoo.ie

The publishers regret that they can enter into no correspondence upon
this matter.

Osprey Publishing supports the Woodland Trust, the UK's leading woodland
conservation charity.

To find out more about our authors and books visit
**www.ospreypublishing.com**. Here you will find extracts, author
interviews, details of forthcoming events and the option to sign up for
our newsletter.

**Key to military symbols**

| | | | | | | |
|---|---|---|---|---|---|---|
| ××××× | ×××× | ××× | ×× | × | III | II |
| Army Group | Army | Corps | Division | Brigade | Regiment | Battalion |
| I | | | | | | |
| Company/Battery | Infantry | Artillery | Cavalry | | | |

**Key to unit identification**

Unit identifier — Commander — Parent unit
(+) with added elements
(–) less elements

**PREVIOUS PAGE**
The restored Theban victory monument (Tropaion) at Leuctra.
(George E. Koronaios, CC0 1.0)

# CONTENTS

# Greece in the early 4th century BC

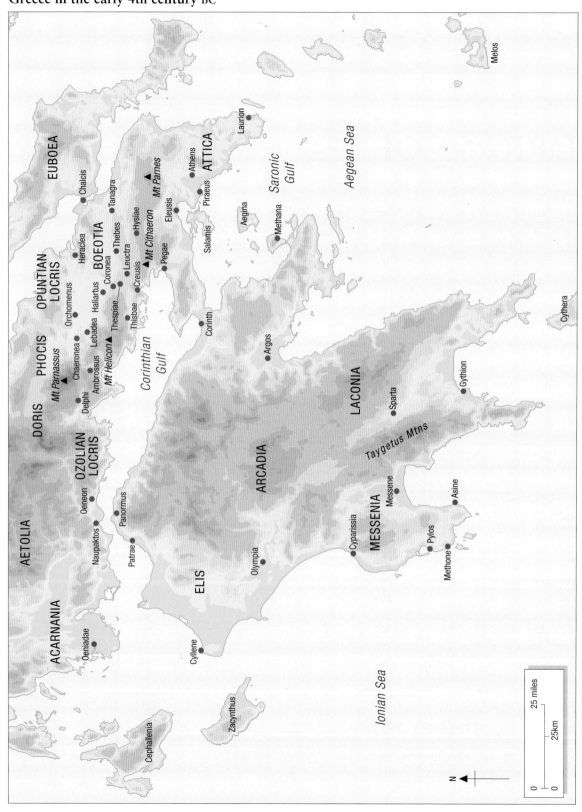

# ORIGINS OF THE CAMPAIGN

The city of Thebes had a rich history in the Greek world stretching back into the depths of antiquity. 'Seven-gated Thebes' was the largest city in Boeotia and dominated the region, although not without ups and downs. Boeotia was a region of Greece through which anyone heading north from Attica or the Peloponnese, and anyone heading south into those regions from the north, would need to travel. Anyone heading to Delphi from the south (unless by sea), for instance, would cross Boeotia, and most probably, go via the inland route through Thebes. It is unsurprising to find that Boeotia and Thebes were a crux of culture and ideas, too, not to mention wars. Boeotia was surrounded and divided by mountains, and by Lake Copais, into two separate regions: the north centred on Orchomenus and the south on Thebes.

This 4th-century BC fragmentary funeral *stele* from Cyrene (now in the Kyrene Museum) shows the essentials of the hoplite panoply in several cities: *aspis*, *dory* and *chlamys*. The subject also wears a sword on his left hip with baldric. Note that the hoplite carries his *dory* in his left hand by the *sauroter*, whilst carrying his *aspis* purely by the *porpax*. (akg-images/ Gilles Mermet)

The flat plains between the ranges and hills of Boeotia were ideal for Greek hoplite warfare, which led Epaminondas to call it 'the dancing floor of war' (Plutarch *Sayings of Kings and Commanders* 18/*Moralia* 193E). It comes as no surprise to find many of the most famous ancient battles were fought in Boeotia (including Plataea, Leuctra, Coronea, Chaeronea, Delium). Several of the cities of Boeotia controlled passes and roads, often the only one into or out of a region, and this made each of them strategically important. Thebes itself, on a ridge of hills and surrounding its low-lying acropolis, the Cadmea, also dominated its environs. The region was fertile and produced crops of high reputation across Greece, which brought prosperity. Despite this, the economy was still agriculturally based and could be crippled by successive bad harvests. Boeotia did not have great mineral resources at its disposal. What is more, the nature of its terrain and the locations of its smaller cities, which dominated passes and were built in commanding and difficult positions, meant that several cities were independently minded and often intractable. This made command and control of a confederacy of Boeotian cities difficult, causing difficulties for Boeotian politics.

The Cadmea citadel at Thebes where the Sacred Band were housed. Thebes had a long history of having elite forces of 300 hoplites stretching back to, at least, the Battle of Plataea in 479 BC (Herodotus 9.67) and Delium in 424 BC (Diodorus 12.70.1), but the *Hieros Lochos* came into their own as a fighting force in the 370s BC, winning the Battle of Tegyra in 375 BC single-handed and leading the Theban charge at Leuctra in 371 BC, both with Pelopidas as their commander. (Nefasdicere, CC BY-SA 3.0)

By the 6th century BC, Thebes had become the dominant city in a loose confederation of several Boeotian cities (Herodotus 6.108). The number of cities fluctuated (probably between eight and 13), and to each of these cities a number of villages or a territory were attached. There were, however, no phratries or tribes in Boeotia, unlike in other Greek states. All Boeotians shared the same dialect and aspects of culture, but, because of the geographical make-up of the region, they were often at loggerheads with one another. The common assembly of the Boeotian federation sat in the Cadmea in Thebes itself. Thebes, the largest and most important city in Boeotia, clearly dominated and essentially controlled the federation through *auctoritas* and harsher methods of control. Thebes' control of the federation is exemplified by Herodotus' use of 'Thebes' when clearly 'Boeotia' is meant (6.108, but also 5.81 and 9.16), and by Thucydides' 'Theban' speech (3.61).

## THE STAIN

Any foreign land invasion of Attica or the Peloponnese needed to go through Boeotia. Should any such invasion prove successful or easy, blame would fall on Boeotia and especially on Thebes. The great stain on Thebes' reputation in the 5th century was that it betrayed Greece and allowed the Persian invaders into Attica in 480 BC. Herodotus especially casts Thebes as a traitor and betrayer of all Greece. In many ways this is unfair (Thebes had little choice but to cooperate with the Persian conquerors) and reflects the (perhaps undeserved) reputation Thebes had following the Greco-Persian Wars. In contrast, many other Greek states had behaved just as Thebes had done (such as Macedon and Thessaly) but escaped blame. The Thebans then fought on the Persian side at the Battle of Plataea in 479 BC, sealing their reputation as traitors. The major opponent of Thebes for most of the next century would be Athens (whose forces opposed the Thebans at Plataea), although even among the Boeotians, Thebes' reputation also suffered (Diodorus 11.81.2).

In the aftermath of the Greco-Persian Wars, when Thebes' domination of any league was understandably much reduced, if not eclipsed entirely, there is still evidence that the Boeotian federation continued. The eclipse of Thebes' reputation and Boeotia's central position meant other powers – Athens and Sparta in particular – began fighting for control of the region.

Sparta had long been seen as the natural leader of Greece, with a reputation for valour and with her hoplites as the epitome of Greek warfare. The victories in the Greco-Persian Wars only enhanced that reputation, although Athens too shared in the glory. The 50 years following the victory at Plataea saw Athens and Sparta come into inevitable conflict over the leadership of Greece and their respective spheres of interest. Sparta was traditionally reluctant to leave the Peloponnese, but Athens was expansionistic and ambitious, and forced Sparta into wider involvement in Greek politics beyond its region.

When offering aid to the Dorians in central Greece against the Phocians in 458–457 BC, the Spartans may have wanted to support Thebes' resurgence and its domination of the Boeotian federation and the region as a counter to the spreading influence of Athens. According to Thucydides (1.108), at the Battle of Tanagra in 457 BC the Spartan army defeated a force from Athens and then returned to the Peloponnese. In contrast, Diodorus' version (11.81.2 – entirely absent from Thucydides) states the Thebans asked the Lacedaemonians to aid them in gaining hegemony over all Boeotia. In return, they offered to make war on Athens. According to Diodorus (11.81.3), the Spartans agreed and sought to set up a Theban-dominated Boeotia and then compelled the cities of Boeotia to join Thebes. Barely two months later, however, the Athenians, in turn, defeated a Boeotian force at Oenophyta and were able to assert control over all of Boeotia, Phocis and parts of Locris, establishing democracies in several Boeotian cities, although they were not able to take Thebes itself. This was part of Athens and Sparta vying for control in the First Peloponnesian War (457–446 BC).

In 447 BC, Thucydides (1.113) recounts that an exiled Boeotian party (including some Thebans) gained possession of Orchomenus and several other towns. This party was presumably the traditional oligarchic or anti-democratic faction that had been ousted by Athens and pro-Athenian forces.

The ruins of the Kabirion, Thebes (home to a secret cult possibly of Phrygian origin). Alexander the Great razed the city in 335 BC and much of the foundations of the 4th-century BC city therefore survive. Thebes bore the brunt of blame for cooperating with the Persians in 480/479 BC, and then was made an example of by Alexander to show what would happen to Greek cities that rebelled against his rule. (DeAgostini/Getty Images)

The Fountain of Dirce in Thebes, another symbol of the city. Dirce was the wife of Lycus, the ruler of Thebes killed by the twins Zethus and Amphion, born to Antiope via Zeus. Where Dirce died, the god Dionysus caused a spring to flow. The outgoing Theban cavalry commander, the *hipparch*, swore in his successor at the site. (DeAgostini/ Getty Images)

These forces defeated the Athenians at the Battle of Coronea in 447 BC and once again established a Theban-dominated Boeotian League. Thebes later claimed responsibility for liberating Boeotia at the battle (Thucydides 3.62). Ostensibly, Thebes and Boeotia now had an ally in Sparta, and in Athens, an enemy whose hatred had grown deeper. It is the constitution following the liberation of Boeotia in 447 BC which most scholars believe the *Hellenica Oxyrhynchia* describes, where Boeotia was divided into 11 districts each with a Boeotarch. This constitution lasted until 387 BC (far longer than other celebrated constitutions or rulers). Despite the fact that the constitution seems to have been designed to minimize Theban power, it did not take Thebes long to assert control. A stable and resurgent Boeotia would necessarily lead to a resurgent Thebes, given it was the seat of assemblies. Alternative locations, such as Orchomenus, were too remote to form the seat of power.

The struggle between Sparta and Athens came to a head in the Second Peloponnesian War (431–404 BC). Indeed, the first act in 431 BC was a Theban attempt on Plataea (Athens' ally) and a Boeotian city that resisted Theban control (Thucydides 2.2–5). Thebes probably expected an easy victory, invited by a pro-Boeotian or anti-Athenian party. Plataea was besieged, and fell in 427 BC, its women sold into slavery. Thucydides makes a point of saying that the ferocity of the Spartan treatment of the Plataeans was down to the Thebans (3.68.4) thinking the Spartans the better ally. Thebans themselves may have repopulated Plataea. If Thebes' treatment of Plataea was anti-Athenian, then the highpoint for Thebes, if not Boeotia, was still to come.

In 424 BC, Athens was riding high in confidence. She had managed to defeat and capture a force of Spartan hoplites on Sphacteria (Thucydides 4.8–38) in 425 BC and was looking to press her advantage. In 424 BC, she moved against Thebes and Boeotia again, but met with disaster at the Battle of Delium (Thucydides 4.93–96). This was the pinnacle of Thebes' revenge against Athens. Athens then suffered a humiliating and crippling defeat in Sicily between 415 and 413 BC (where the Boeotians sent a force to oppose the Athenians – Thucydides 7.19.3). This defeat led to reinvigorated attacks on Attica by the Spartans with Boeotia and Thebes as their allies. In return, Thebes became wealthy from plundering Attica and even seized additional territory. One Theban even suggested razing Athens (Pausanias 10.9.9). Soon, however, it was clear that Sparta posed just as great a threat to Theban and Boeotian autonomy, and paradoxically, Athens would become Thebes' ally against Sparta.

Victory in the Second Peloponnesian War saw the establishment of the Spartan hegemony, a period that saw Sparta dominate the politics of the rest of Greece in a more actively interventionist way than in the previous century (and which ended at the Battle of Leuctra). Spartan armies were often abroad and Spartan garrisons and pro-Spartan governments were installed in various Greek cities. Pro-independence movements in many of these cities therefore shared common ground even when they had been bitter enemies previously.

As Sparta emerged victorious in the Second Peloponnesian War, a cooling of relations with Thebes was evident. Sparta refused to destroy Athens, and, perhaps an indicator of a change of leadership at Thebes, factions emerged arguing that the Boeotians had been too pro-Spartan. Ismenias, Antitheos and Androcleidas supported a more pro-Athenian stance against the incumbent, pro-Spartan faction of Leontiades, Asias and Koiratadas (*Hellenica Oxyrhynchia* 17.1–2). Thebes now saw Sparta as a threat to her independence and was soon harbouring Athenian exiles.

Between the end of the Second Peloponnesian War in 404 BC and the outbreak of the Corinthian War in 395 BC, major disagreements in our sources appear. Thebes and Boeotia, however, grew increasingly hostile towards Sparta. Thebes refused to send a force against Athens in 404–403 BC (Xenophon *Hellenica* 2.4.30) and stood by when democracy was restored. In 400–399 BC, the Boeotian League refused to join a Spartan expedition against Elis (*Hellenica* 3.2.21–25) and in 397 BC refused to send troops with the Spartan king Agesilaus II against Persia. The Spartans still had allies in Phocis and the Boeotians in Locris, and this led to territory disputes. Xenophon (*Hellenica* 3.5.1–5) claims that the Boeotian leaders were bribed by Persian gold to make war on Sparta. The Persians wanted Agesilaus out of Persia, so a war in Greece that embroiled Sparta was the perfect pretext. This

The Cadmea citadel was named after the legendary founder of Thebes, Cadmus. It has remains dating back at least to the Mycenean period and was a prestigious part of the city. Housing the Sacred Band there connected them to the city's identity (and the expulsion of the Spartan garrison who took up residence there), together with their swearing of oaths at other important locations (such as the Shrine of Iolaus, the nephew of Heracles). (DeAgostini/Getty Images)

bribe is contradicted by Pausanias (3.9.3–8) and the *Hellenica Oxyrhynchia* (18). Boeotian forces invaded Phocis, and Sparta in turn provided aid to the Phocians. Thebes also sent to Athens an offer of alliance (*Hellenica* 3.5.7–17). The offer was accepted by the Athenians unanimously – a reversal of alliances and enmities from only a decade before. Orchomenus, however, revolted against Theban leadership (Plutarch *Pelopidas* 16.1; *Lysander* 28.2; Xenophon *Hellenica* 3.5.6). Soon the Spartan commander Lysander would meet his death in battle at Haliartus in 395 BC. The other Spartan general, Pausanias, arrived, but the Boeotians, reinforced by the Athenians, were too strong and a truce was arranged. In the winter of 395 BC, a meeting between the Boeotians, Athenians, Argives and Corinthians at Corinth decided upon a grand alliance against Sparta (Diodorus 14.82.1–4). Many smaller states joined and several Spartan allies revolted. The Boeotians fought a successful battle against the Phocians at Naryx (Diodorus 14.82.7–10).

News of all these developments forced Agesilaus to return to Greece from Persia, marching through Thessaly in 394 BC. The Spartans concentrated their forces under the general Aristodemus (King Agesipolis being still a minor) and prepared to meet those of the alliance; the two forces met at the Battle of Nemea, 4km west of Corinth. The resultant Spartan victory was not decisive. Although the alliance troops fled, the Boeotians had been victorious against the Spartan left wing. Agesilaus soon arrived in Boeotia, possibly unexpectedly since no serious force opposed him. Agesilaus faced the alliance at Coronea (perhaps only a month after Nemea), reinforced by troops from Orchomenus and Phocis (*Hellenica* 4.3.15). Again, the Spartans won, but not decisively, and the war continued into 393 BC. In 392 BC, a democratic revolt in Corinth further strengthened support for the alliance, although a counter-revolution admitted a Spartan garrison into the city. A Boeotian garrison in Lechaeum was wiped out (*Hellenica* 4.4.12). Attempts at peace negotiations proved fruitless, and in 391 BC Lechaeum was recaptured by the alliance (Diodorus 14.86.40) and the Athenian general Iphicrates was able to destroy a Spartan *mora* of 600 men using mostly lightly armed *peltasts* (*Hellenica* 4.5.11–17, Plutarch *Agesilaus* 22.2). The war turned against the

The relatively flat terrain of Boeotia reveals why it was known as the 'dancing floor of war' (Plutarch *Sayings of Kings and Commanders* 18) and why so many battles were fought on its plains. Indeed, hoplite warfare was best suited to such terrain, something most other parts of Greece lacked. Boeotia was also a highway for any Greeks travelling north from Attica or the Peloponnese, or south from the rest of Greece, and so the many wars fought in Boeotia, and for control of it, should not surprise us. (DEA/ARCHIVIO J. LANGE/ DeAgostini/Getty Images)

A detail of the combat scene on the Tomb of Payava. We can see that the *peltasts* wear *exomis* tunics only (the middle figure is naked) and they carry *pelte* shields (a smaller round shield than the *aspis*) and wear *pilos* helmets (the right-most example has a crest). Light-armed *peltasts* from Athens had shown the vulnerability of the Spartan *mora* at the Battle of Lechaeum in 391 BC. (Photograph by Mike Peel (www.mikepeel.net), CC BY-SA 4.0)

alliance in 388 BC, and in 387 BC the Persians, who had been bankrolling the alliance's activities against Sparta, now sided with the Spartans and their admiral Antalcidas. The Athenians sued for peace (*Hellenica* 5.1.25–29) and Corinth and Argos were also willing. Only Boeotia was left beligerent, and Agesilaus demanded that Thebes swear that all Boeotian cities would be autonomous, or the entire Spartan levy would invade Boeotia. The Boeotians, alone and now without allies, were forced to agree, and the Boeotian League collapsed into the independent towns that had made it.

This was a crippling blow to Thebes' power, but also to the collective power of the Boeotian League. Several of the governments set up in Boeotia were pro-Spartan or saw pro-Spartan parties come to the fore. Some Thebans served in Spartan armies after 387 BC, especially at Mantinea in 385 BC, although there was a growing desire in the city (led by Ismenias) for it to reassert itself (*Hellenica* 5.2.25). There may also have been a pro-Spartan group (led by Leontiades) who wanted to maintain (Spartan-supported) power. In 382 BC, the Spartans intervened in Thebes directly, although the circumstances are reported differently in our sources. The Spartan commander Phoibidas seized the Cadmea in Thebes (Diodorus 15.20.2) and had Ismenias executed. This could have been a Spartan policy (Diodorus 15.19.3, 15.20.2; Plutarch *Pelopidas* 5.1) although Xenophon claims Phoibidas acted alone rather than in accordance with wider Spartan ideology (*Hellenica* 5.2.27–28). Three hundred Thebans were exiled (Diodorus 15.20.2 – Xenophon claims they retired, *Hellenica* 5.2.31) to Athens. Phoibidas was fined, but the Spartan garrison remained – the Spartans punished the man who committed the crime but approved of the crime itself. Xenophon plays up the idea that all this was the fault of a local party at Thebes led by Leontiades. A pro-Spartan government was set up in Thebes led by Leontiades, supported by 1,500 Spartan troops, although this number is probably far too high (Diodorus 15.25.3, Plutarch *Pelopidas* 12.3, 13.2). Other Boeotian cities soon endured similar brutal governments (Plutarch *Agesilaus* 24.1, *Hellenica* 5.4.1–2).

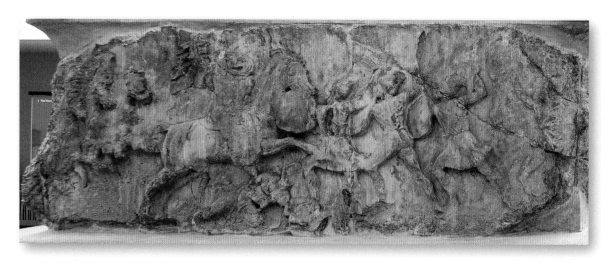

The full battle scene from the Tomb of Payava shows lightly armed *peltasts* fighting cavalry. A traditional tomb could combine old-fashioned elements with modern depictions. Lightly armed troops had always been present in Greek warfare, but their role is not usually emphasized in the sources; Leuctra is no different. (Photograph by Mike Peel (www.mikepeel.net), CC BY-SA 4.0)

The Theban exiles in Athens smouldered in resentment. The Spartans ordered the Athenians to expel the exiles; an order Athens ignored. How Thebes was restored and the pro-Spartan tyranny expelled is another case of our sources disagreeing. A small group of exiles returned to Thebes, assassinated key members of the tyranny and restored Theban government, installing a democracy. The Spartan garrison was besieged, then (at some point) surrendered and was allowed to depart. Among the Theban exiles was Pelopidas. Four new Boeotarchs were elected and they declared their intent of restoring the Boeotian League, although on a democratic model (*Pelopidas* 13.1, 14.1). The Spartan garrisons of Plataea and Thespiae were called upon, but could do nothing. A new alliance with Athens was forged.

It did not take long for the Spartans to attempt to wrestle back control of Thebes. King Cleombrotus was dispatched commanding a force (his first as king) in early 378 BC (*Hellenica* 5.4.14). He reached Thespiae via Plataea, stayed 16 days and then retired. Cleombrotus was criticized for his inaction (5.4.16), although around the same time, Athens was convinced to distance itself from Thebes (5.4.19, 22). Very quickly, however, the concord between Athens and Sparta fell apart and Athens formed the Second Athenian Confederacy to secure freedom from Sparta, which Thebes promptly joined (Diodorus 15.28.2–3, 29.7; *Pelopidas* 15.1; Xenophon is silent on the confederacy, although he does state Thebes and Athens entered an alliance, *Hellenica* 5.4.34). Thebes was fortified, and by June, Agesilaus was in the field against it with five-sixths of Sparta's manpower (Diodorus 15.32.1). Troops from Thebes and Athens saw him off without a major engagement, but Spartan garrisons continued to raid Theban territory.

The desire of several Boeotian cities to overthrow their Spartan masters and join the newly resurgent Thebes was growing. Agesilaus came again in 377 BC, but again declined to fight a set battle against the Thebans and Athenians. In 376 BC, Cleombrotus took the field against Thebes, but was blocked at Mt Cithaeron and the following year Thebes began to bring other cities over to its side (*Hellenica* 5.4.63). These probably included Tanagra, Haliartus, Lebadea, Coronea and Chaeronea. In 375 BC, the Thebans moved against Orchomenus. As they retreated from this advance, Pelopidas and the Sacred Band would clash with a much larger force of two Spartan *morai* at the Battle of Tegyra. The outcome would provide a shock to the idea of Spartan invincibility on the field of battle.

# CHRONOLOGY

All dates refer to BC.

| | |
|---|---|
| 447 | Battle of Coronea (First Peloponnesian War) – Boeotian victory over Athens. Boeotian League reconstituted, dominated by Thebes. |
| 413–404 | Thebes allied with Sparta in the Decelean phase of Second Peloponnesian War (431–404). |
| 404–371 | Spartan hegemony over Greece. |
| 404/403 | Thebes refuses to send a force against Athens. |
| 400/399 | Boeotian League refuses to join Spartan expedition to Elis. |
| 397 | Boeotian League refuses to join Spartan King Agesilaus II's expedition to Persia. |
| 395–387 | Corinthian War. |
| 395 | Summer: Battle of Haliartus, Theban and Haliartan victory over Sparta.<br>Winter: Grand Alliance between Boeotia, Athens, Corinth and Argos against Sparta. |
| 394 | Battle of Naryx: Boeotian victory over Sparta's ally Phocis.<br>Agesilaus marches towards Greece from Persia.<br>Battle of Nemea: indecisive Spartan victory over Grand Alliance.<br>Battle of Coronea: indecisive Spartan victory over Grand Alliance. |
| 392 | Coup and counter-coup in Corinth; city occupied by Spartan garrison. |
| 391 | Battle of Lechaeum: Athenian victory over Spartans. |
| 387 | Athens, Corinth and Argos make peace with Sparta (the King's Peace). Boeotian League dissolved into independent cities. |
| 385 | Boeotians serve at Spartan siege of Mantinea. |
| 382 | Spartans occupy Theban acropolis, pro-Spartan government installed. Anti-government leaders exiled to Athens or put to death. |
| 380 | Cleombrotus I becomes co-ruler (alongside Agesilaus II) of Sparta. |
| 379 | Small group of Theban exiles return to Thebes; restoration of pro-Boeotian government.<br>Spartan garrison in Thebes' Cadmea put under siege. |
| 378–371 | Boeotian War. |
| 378 | Early: Cleombrotus leads an expedition into Boeotia, to Thespiae and Plataea.<br>Second Athenian Confederacy to secure Greek freedom against Sparta; Thebes joins. |

## Boeotia and its battle sites

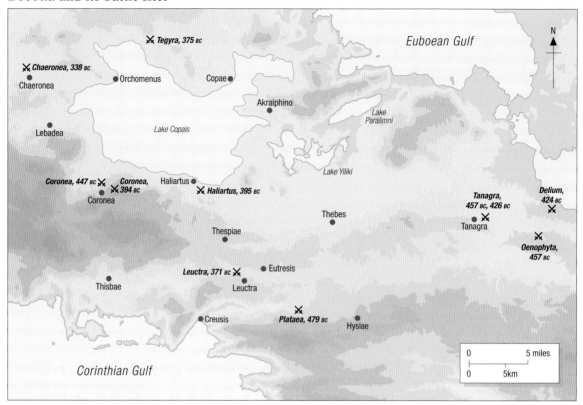

| 378–377 | Agesilaus invades Boeotia twice, skirmishing against Theban and Athenian troops – but no major engagements. |
|---|---|
| 376 | Cleombrotus attempts to invade Boeotia, turned back at Mt Cithaeron. |
| 375 | Several Boeotian cities expel their Spartan garrisons and join Thebes.<br>Summer: Battle of Tegyra – Theban victory against Spartans.<br>Thebans invade Phocis.<br>Cleombrotus dispatched with Spartan force to reinforce Phocis, Thebans withdraw.<br>Late: peace agreed between Athens, Sparta and their allies. |
| 374 | Thebes continues to take cities. |
| 371 | Cleombrotus dispatched with Spartan force to reinforce Phocis against Jason of Pherae, Thebes' ally.<br>Peace conference at Sparta. Thebes attempts to change the terms of their signature. Agesilaus refuses.<br>Cleombrotus invades Boeotia from Phocis, makes his way to Leuctra.<br>Battle of Leuctra. |
| 371–362 | Theban hegemony over Greece. |

# THE BATTLE OF TEGYRA 375 BC

Once Thebes had broken free of Spartan domination following the King's Peace in 379/378 BC, it set about 'freeing' the other cities of Boeotia of their Spartan garrisons. Soon, only the garrison at Orchomenus remained, and Pelopidas (learning the garrison had moved against Opuntian Locris) set out for Orchomenus with the Sacred Band and a few horsemen (Plutarch *Pelopidas* 16.2). Diodorus gives the total number as 500 men (15.37.1). When the Thebans got to the city, however, they found another Spartan force in place, and so set out to return to Thebes. The Melas River (probably the modern Cephissus/Kiphisos, which originally drained into Lake Copais) was in flood, and so Pelopidas was forced to return to Thebes by the more circuitous route along the northern edge of Lake Copais. At Tegyra, Pelopidas' force encountered the Spartan garrison returning from Locris.

The Boeotian Cephissus (or Kiphisos) River is the probable candidate for Plutarch's Melas River (*Pelopidas* 16.3). Plutarch tells us that it flooded the plain on the return route from Orchomenus to Thebes and so Pelopidas was forced to skirt around Lake Copais to the north. By doing so, he encountered the Spartan force returning from Locris. (Costas78, CC BY-SA 3.0)

# The approach to Tegyra, 375 BC

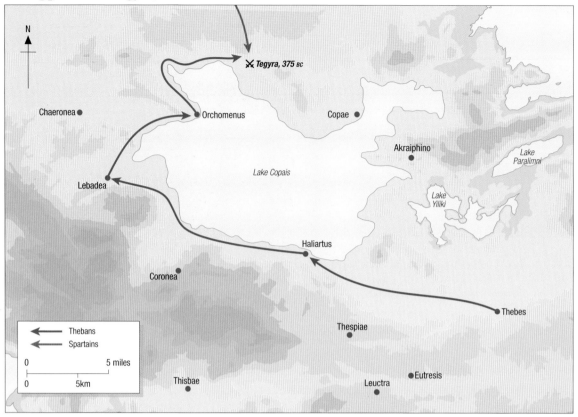

Although the exact location of the Battle of Tegyra is debated, the narrow pass at which the Thebans encountered the returning Spartans can only be a few places. Buck (1979, p. 8) places the site at modern Polyira (6km directly north of Orchomenus) as it has a Mycenean temple ruin, or Pyrgos. For our reconstruction, we have chosen the pass just north of Pyrgos as the site of the battle. Plutarch tells us (*Pelopidas* 16.2-17.1) the battle was fought in the district of Tegyra, named after the temple to Apollo Tegyraeus, which had been abandoned by the 4th century BC but which had been active during the Greco-Persian Wars (490–479 BC). The site is a narrow pass, had two springs and was near to the Ptoion Mountains, the range on the eastern shore of the lake, running from Akraiphino (opposite Orchomenus) eastwards to the Gulf of Euboea – and so 'near' is a relative term. The site should be located on the northern shore, on the route from Locris to Orchomenus and, it would seem, the battle could be seen from the acropolis of Orchomenus. The road also needed to lead towards Thebes. The site we have chosen fits these criteria: it is a narrow pass, it leads from Locris and, beyond the pass, the road branches eastwards towards Thebes.

The Spartan garrison force returning from Locris vastly outnumbered the Thebans. Diodorus tells us (15.37.1) that they were twice the Thebans in number, whereas Plutarch (*Pelopidas* 16.1) tells us there were two *morai* of Spartans, therefore between 1,000 and 1,800 men (based on the sources he gives). Modern calculations of a *mora* 600-strong would still make this

1,200 Spartans versus 500 Thebans, 200 of them cavalry. Plutarch here shows how many sources he was using (Ephorus, Callisthenes, Polybius and other writers).

According to Plutarch (*Pelopidas* 17.1–2), as the Thebans entered the narrow pass, a man ran up to Pelopidas and cried that they had fallen into their enemies' hands. Pelopidas' response 'Why not they into ours?' fits with the tradition of pithy statements by ancient commanders. Pelopidas ordered all the cavalry up from the rear and put the 300 into close array (*synegagen*). They would charge the Spartans. This passage seems misleading and more than one editor, translator and commentator has interpreted it to mean that the cavalry were in front of the Sacred Band and would lead the charge (Georgiadou 1997, p. 149; Buck 1994, p. 99). This

A silver stater from Opuntian Locris dated to between 380 and 360 BC depicting Ajax, son of Oileus. Pelopidas met the Spartan garrison returning from Locris in 375 BC at Tegyra. The coin shows details of the interior of an *aspis* as well as the Corinthian helmet and the cloak wrapped around the left forearm (now in the Metropolitan Museum L.1999.19.80 (ANS 1967.152.247)). (Marie-Lan Nguyen, CC BY 2.5)

was not the role of ancient cavalry, and cavalry would not charge the solid shield-wall of the Spartan phalanx. As would recur at Leuctra, it is more likely that the Sacred Band would lead the charge, cutting its way through the enemy; and the cavalry would follow the infantry, perhaps chasing down any who fled. Positioned behind the 300, the cavalry might also dissuade any attempt at outflanking the small hoplite force; any move by the Spartans to do that might expose their own vulnerable flank to the Theban cavalry.

The only discrepancy between Plutarch and Diodorus is that the latter says the Thebans were attacking the Spartans (15.37.1) whereas Plutarch states (*Pelopidas* 17.3) that the Spartans, confident of victory, advanced against the Thebans. It would seem more likely that the Thebans attacked rather than waiting for the Spartan advance. Pelopidas would lead the attack again at Leuctra, and here, by attacking and fighting at a point of his own choosing, Pelopidas would avoid being surrounded and cut down. There is a confidence in Pelopidas' action at Tegyra that suggests he had a plan even when faced by a superior number of Spartan adversaries. It is possible that both sides advanced against one another simultaneously (just as they did at Leuctra according to Diodorus, 15.55.3).

The onset was at the point where the Spartan commanders, Gorgoleon and Theopompus, were stationed, and they, understandably, were confident of victory. Pelopidas was in the front rank of the 300, just as he would be at Leuctra. The point of impact indicates that the Thebans attacked on the Spartan right, where the commanders would have been stationed. Both were polemarchs and so commanded a *mora* each, but both seem to have been stationed together (perhaps to represent their equal status). Plutarch continues (*Pelopidas* 17.3) that the polemarchs clashed with Pelopidas and fell. Possibly, therefore, Pelopidas positioned himself so that he personally would contend with the Spartan commanders in the front rank (again suggesting a definite plan). Once the Spartan leaders had fallen, the entire Spartan force were seized

**TO ORCHOMENUS**

**THEBAN/BOEOTIAN**
1. Sacred Band
2. Cavalry

xxxx

**PELOPIDAS**

## ▼ EVENTS

**1.** Both sides enter the narrow pass at the same time, each from the opposite direction.

**2.** As soon as the Spartan force is seen at the other end of the pass, Pelopidas draws up the Sacred Band into close order. His cavalry force is drawn up behind them. Pelopidas himself takes up position in the front rank of the Sacred Band.

**3.** The Spartans draw up their two *morai* (each of approximately 600 men) abreast. The polemarchs Gorgoleon and Theopompos take position in the centre of the right *mora*.

**4.** As soon as the troops are deployed in formation, Pelopidas charges the Sacred Band towards the position where the Spartan commanders are stationed in the centre of the right Spartan *mora*.

**5.** After fierce fighting, Theopompus and Gorgoleon fall, along with those around them.

**6.** The remaining Spartans open up a lane to allow the Thebans to proceed on their way. Pelopidas enters the opening, but uses it to attack the remaining Spartans.

**7.** Soon the Spartans flee from the battle wholesale towards Orchomenus. The Thebans only pursue them a little way, fearing that a relief force could arrive from Orchomenus. They return to set up a trophy, and then continue home towards Thebes.

# THE BATTLE OF TEGYRA, 375 BC

The small Theban force led by Pelopidas consisting of the Sacred Band and a few cavalry (Plutarch *Pelopidas* 16.2), 500 men in all according to Diodorus (15.37.1), marched from Thebes to Orchomenus hoping to free the city from its Spartan garrison. When they found another garrison in place, they made to return to Thebes, but the Melas River was in flood and they could not go back the way they came. Instead, they marched around the northern edge of Lake Copais. In the region of Tegyra, Pelopidas' force encountered the Spartan garrison returning from Locris. In the resulting battle, a superior Lacedaemonian force was defeated by an enemy of inferior numbers for the first time. Tegyra showed that Sparta alone did not produce superior fighting men.

GORGOLEON/
THEOPOMPOS

TO LOCRIS

TO THEBES

**SPARTAN**
A. Two Spartan *morai*
(600 men each)

N

Note: gridlines are shown at intervals of 100m (109 yards)

## PELOPIDAS AND THE SACRED BAND AT THE BATTLE OF TEGYRA, 375 BC (PP. 20–21)

Pelopidas leads the Sacred Band (**1**) in its charge into the right of the Spartan formation (**2**), where the Spartan commanders Gorgoleon and Theopompus are stationed. Theban elites of 300 soldiers have a long history of forming the front line of Theban and Boeotian attacks stretching back at least to the Battle of Plataea in 479 BC. The tactic of targeting an enemy commander had also been attempted successfully before (such as at Haliartus in 395 BC) although not specifically by an elite force. The Sacred Band are 25 shields across and 12 ranks deep, attacking a Spartan formation at least twice their total size, 150 shields across but only eight ranks deep. Behind the Sacred Band, 200 Theban cavalry (**3**) fan out to prevent the remaining Spartan forces from attempting to encircle the smaller Theban force. They will follow up the charge of the Sacred Band and chase down any Spartans who flee. The compact Theban formation suits the narrow pass of Tegyra and allows the smaller Theban force to concentrate on a single point in the Spartan lines rather than spread their line to the width of their enemy (a more usual tactic) and risk being overwhelmed.

The Thebans have *aspis* shields (**4**) decorated with the club of Heracles (an emblem of Thebes, and the shrine of Iolaus – nephew of Heracles – was where Sacred Band members swore their oaths). All wield *dory* spears with a leaf-shaped tip and bear *xiphos* or *kopis* swords on their left hips, suspended on baldrics over their right shoulders. The Theban cavalry are lightly armoured, wearing tunics, cloaks and *petasos* hats.

The two *morai* of Spartans wear the red cloak (an emblem of their citizenship) and carry *aspis* shields and wear a variety of different armours. They, too, carry *dory* spears (although theirs are shorter, at 2.4m). Likewise, Spartan swords were shorter than those in other Greek states. A Spartan commander can be seen with his distinctive transverse crest (**5**). The Spartans famously fought barefooted, and it is possible the Thebans did too – several aspects of the training of the Sacred Band seem to have been for the Thebans to familiarize themselves with Spartan techniques in order to be able to overcome them in battle. These probably involved some type of emulation.

with fear and opened a lane in the *mora* for the Thebans to pass through. Pelopidas, however, used the lane to press his attack further, and the Spartans broke and fled towards Orchomenus (that is, in the direction from which the Thebans had attacked). Plutarch states (*Pelopidas* 17.4–5) that the Thebans were in fear of a relief force coming from nearby Orchomenus, and so did not pursue the Spartans far.

We are given no number for casualties. The two Spartan commanders, Gorgoleon and Theopompus, and those about them, were killed (*Pelopidas* 17.3–4). More were slain when the Thebans passed through the corridor made for them. Diodorus gives no number of casualties, but talks (15.37.1) of the Spartans being defeated (for the first time) by a smaller number of enemy troops.

## THE LESSON OF TEGYRA

The Spartans had betrayed their very own code of conduct by fleeing from battle. More than that, however, the Spartans had outnumbered the enemy. The Thebans set up a trophy and set off home. Plutarch's summary (*Pelopidas* 17.5–6) is that never before had the Spartans been overpowered by an inferior number of enemies. Tegyra was the first battle in which other Greeks learned that it was not Sparta alone who produced warlike men who were courageous and shunned danger. These were the very skills Epaminondas and Pelopidas were aiming to instil in their forces, and Tegyra served as the perfect test.

The Acropolis of Orchomenus commands views of the surrounding countryside. Pelopidas' limited pursuit after Tegyra, for fear of reinforcements coming from the city, is understandable – it is entirely possible that the battle was visible from the city walls. (Gerhard Haubold, CC BY-SA 3.0)

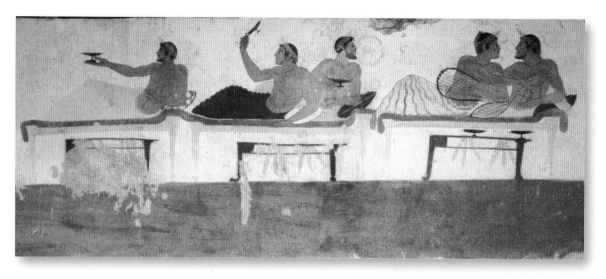

A 5th-century BC fresco of a symposium from the Tomb of the Divers, Paestum, Italy. The formation of the Sacred Band at Thebes may provide vital dating evidence for the composition of the *Symposium* dialogue of Plato. In it (178E–179A), Plato claims that with an army of lovers, a small band might conquer the world. This might place the dialogue after the dramatic achievements of the Sacred Band at Tegyra in 375 BC. (PHAS/Universal Images Group via Getty Images)

Plutarch exaggerates slightly, for some of the lessons at Tegyra might have already been taught. At the Battle of Haliartus in 395 BC (*Hellenica* 3.5.5–8 and 17–22, Plutarch *Lysander* 28), the Thebans defeated the Spartans under Lysander. The Thebans rushed to Haliartus against a Spartan invasion, and when Lysander arrived ahead of the other Spartan force led by Pausanias, he attacked the city without waiting. According to Xenophon, the Thebans did not hesitate to attack but came on at a run with both infantry and cavalry (*Hellenica* 3.5.19) – suggestive for both Tegyra and Leuctra – and Lysander seems to have been targeted and was killed. When Lysander was cut down, the Spartan forces broke and fled. Plutarch's version (*Lysander* 28.5–6) has Lysander advance against the city and the Thebans (drawn up for battle inside the city) remained inactive until Lysander was within striking distance. Then they opened the gates and charged directly at Lysander, killing him, his soothsayer and a few companions. There may have been lessons here which Epaminondas and Pelopidas seized upon – notably the decisive charge against the enemy leaders.

Even the lesson of a numerically inferior force defeating a greater force may have been remembered. At Munychia in 404 BC, a confident and emboldened Athenian force had defeated a numerically superior one of Spartans and oligarchic supporters (*Hellenica* 2.4.2–12, 19). Despite these lessons, even the ancient sources saw Tegyra as a prelude to Leuctra. Plutarch begins his account of Tegyra (*Pelopidas* 16.1) by saying, portentously, exactly that. He adds that it was Pelopidas' victory alone, and one that gave the Spartans no excuse for their defeat. Likewise, Diodorus gives his summation of events at Tegyra a portentous feel (15.37.1–2), stating that such a thing had never occurred before (a numerically inferior force defeating a superior Spartan one), and that in the past it was glory enough to defeat a Spartan force, even if the victors had outnumbered the Spartans.

We will see that Pelopidas massing his troops and focussing his attack on the position of the Spartan commanders on the enemy right were tactics that would be deliberately repeated at Leuctra, lessons learned from the history of Spartan defeats.

It is little wonder that there is no mention of the defeat of Tegyra in Xenophon at all. If the Battle of Lechaeum was a 'disaster' (*Hellenica* 4.5.7) (when a single *mora* was defeated by the Athenian general Iphicrates), then Tegyra was a catastrophe, with no words for the scale of the disaster that was to follow at Leuctra. All of this makes Xenophon's description of Leuctra as a 'disaster' a massive understatement. His silence on Tegyra occurs at the end of Book 5 of the *Hellenica* (5.52–66). The opening of Book 6 (6.1) simply reports that the Thebans subdued the cities of Boeotia then made an expedition to Phocis. In his account of the Battle of Tegyra (*Pelopidas* 17.2), Plutarch tells us that he used Ephorus, Callisthenes and Polybius as sources. It is worth noting that Xenophon's *Hellenica* is not mentioned here by Plutarch even though he was aware of Xenophon's works, and Plutarch's near contemporary Arrian went so far in his dedication to Xenophon to call himself by that name and call his history of Alexander the *Anabasis* in direct emulation of Xenophon's own *Anabasis*.

The Athenian philosopher Plato may have noted the importance of what happened at Tegyra. In his *Symposium* (178E–179A), he suggests that an army composed of lovers, as the Sacred Band was, might be best for a city's protection, and that such a 'little band' might be victorious all over the world. The dating of the *Symposium* is tricky, usually to around 378 BC (which makes such comments intriguing). James DeVoto (1992, pp. 3–19), however, has argued that this Plato passage post-dates Tegyra and the actions of the Sacred Band at that battle may have inspired it. It is certainly worth considering.

Diodorus' parting comment (15.37.2) on the Battle of Tegyra is telling: Thebes swelled with pride and her men became renowned for their valour. What is more, they had put themselves in a prime position to compete for the supremacy of Greece. Thebes had shown that she had learned the lessons of the past and had put the solutions devised by Epaminondas and Pelopidas into practice at the Battle of Tegyra in 375 BC. Thebes was confident of her own abilities and her own hoplites against those vaunted men of Sparta, and had shown that the idea of Spartan invincibility was a myth. Indeed, Tegyra had shown that the idea of the superiority of Spartans in battle or as hoplites was more a weakness in the mindset of her opponents.

# FROM TEGYRA TO LEUCTRA, 375–371 BC

Following the Theban victory at the Battle of Tegyra, the Thebans invaded Phocis, Sparta's ally. This prompted a new expedition, again commanded by Cleombrotus, but the Thebans retreated to the passes into Boeotia.

Athens was becoming suspicious of Theban intentions to make all of Boeotia Theban, and in late 375 BC peace was agreed between Athens, Sparta and their allies. Again, our sources disagree and cannot be reconciled (Diodorus 15.38, Xenophon *Hellenica* 6.2.1). Thebes, led by Epaminondas, refused to sign the peace (according to Diodorus) although Sparta did withdraw its garrisons from Plataea, Thespiae and Orchomenus, which implies Boeotia was party to the peace terms. Soon, Thebes moved against Plataea (Pausanias 9.1.4–8), Thespiae (Diodorus 15.46.6; *Hellenica* 6.4.10) and Tanagra. Orchomenus would capitulate after Leuctra (Diodorus 15.57.1), becoming an ally (and not a full member of the League).

In 371 BC, another attempt at peace was made, all sides having been at war since 378 BC. A conference was to be held at Sparta. Cleombrotus was in Phocis with a Spartan force to secure it from the attentions of Boeotia's ally Jason of Pherae. A treaty was drawn up and signed by Sparta on behalf of herself and her allies, and by Athens and the cities of the Athenian Confederacy (*Hellenica* 6.3.19–20). The following day, however, Epaminondas (Xenophon only mentions 'the Thebans') asked to change their signature to indicate that the Boeotians (and not just the Thebans) had sworn. Agesilaus refused and Thebes' name was struck from the treaty. There was peace between all other Greek states except between Sparta and Thebes. Cleombrotus was in Phocis with a sizeable force, and war was about to be renewed.

The Funerary *naiskos* (free-standing temple) of Aristonautes, from the Keramikos in Athens (now in the Archaeological Museum of Athens (Inv. 738). Dating to 350–325 BC, it shows the young soldier whose father, Archenautes, and *deme*, Halai, are named as required at Athens. He wears a muscled cuirass, cloak and short *pteruges*. He carries an *aspis* shield and wears a *pilos* or Phrygian helmet. He probably originally carried a spear (he wears no sword), but his right forearm is lost. (Marsyas, CC BY-SA 3.0)

# THE BATTLE OF LEUCTRA 371 BC

## OPPOSING COMMANDERS

### Spartan commanders

Our information on the Spartan command structure in the early 4th century BC is limited to only a few sources. In many cases the historians of the period simply mention the Spartans (or Lacedaemonians). Sparta had a unique dual hereditary kingship, whereby two families, the Agaids and the Eurypontids, held the throne. In terms of military duties, if one king led an expedition, the other would stay at home. At Leuctra, the Agiad king, **Cleombrotus I**, led the army while the more experienced and older Eurypontid **Agesilaus II** remained in Sparta.

Agesilaus had been king since 398 BC, militarily active before that, and would reign until 360 BC. He was the primary reason for Sparta's survival after the disaster at Leuctra (and he would oppose continued Theban attempts to further overthrow Sparta with immense energy until the (second) Battle of Mantinea in 362 BC). Agesilaus was an experienced commander and so his ceding command to Cleombrotus in 371 BC was peculiar, although in 376 BC we are told he was confined to his bed (*Hellenica* 5.4.58) and that after Leuctra he still had not recovered from illness (6.4.18). Cleombrotus had been king only since 380 BC, although very little is known about him, and he does not feature greatly in our sources.

There were, however, checks on a king's power at Sparta. The kings were simply two members of the *Gerousia* council and the magistrates (Ephors) could also curb the power of the kings. Thus, when Cleombrotus commanded Spartan armies against Thebes in 378 BC (*Hellenica* 5.4.14–16), and did not press his advantage against Thebes itself, command of the army was taken from him and given to Agesilaus. He was suspected of doing as little damage against Thebes as he could (5.4.16). Cleombrotus again commanded against the Thebans in 376 BC (*Hellenica* 5.4.59); on that occasion, he was easily turned back from the pass by a Theban and Athenian garrison. In 374 BC, he was

There is no surviving archaeological record of Spartan shields depicting Lambda (Λ) but we have a fragment from a Greek play telling us they did (Eupolis fragment 394). We do have other cities (such as Athens) and Sikyon who used Sigma (Σ). Xenophon, *Hellenica* 4.4.10, tells of the Spartans borrowing Sikyonian shields and the Argives, thinking they were from the latter city, came against them with confidence. (Photo12/Universal Images Group via Getty Images)

This Spartan bronze shield covering, captured at the Battle of Pylos in 425 BC and dedicated in the Athenian Agora (now in the Ancient Agora Museum in Athens), would have remained similar to the shield coverings used by the Spartans at Leuctra in 371 BC. (Giovanni Dall'Orto via Wikimedia Commons)

in command of two-thirds of the Spartan forces – four *morai* – to aid Phocis. Even at the start of the Leuctra account (*Hellenica* 6.4.5), we find a speech (rather, a thinly veiled threat) addressed to Cleombrotus that if he ever wanted to see his homeland again, he should do battle with the Thebans.

In 371 BC, Cleombrotus was in Phocis according to Xenophon (*Hellenica* 6.4.2), and, after peace was made, he asked for instructions from Sparta. Rather than disband his army, he was instructed to lead the army against the Thebans at once (6.4.3), and took his army into Boeotia. He did not enter from Phocis where the pass was guarded, but proceeded to Thisbae, and from there, by a mountainous and unexpected route (6.4.4), to Creusis. He then marched to Leuctra in the territory of Thespiae. From Diodorus (15.52.1) we learn he was at Coronea and that Epaminondas marched to seize that pass (15.52.7). Diodorus does not give the route of Cleombrotus, but tells us (15.53.1) that he entered Boeotia without danger; although he reports ten triremes taken along the route, while Xenophon mentions his taking 12 at Creusis (*Hellenica* 6.4.4).

The Spartan order of battle was a conservative one, and the training of her hoplites had always concentrated on drill and discipline. This makes the confusion within the Spartan ranks of Plutarch's account of Leuctra (*Pelopidas* 23.2) seem unlikely. We find that the Spartans drew up their line in a traditional way, with Cleombrotus on the right as was customary. Diodorus opens his account (15.55.1) by telling us that Cleombrotus and Archidamus (son of Agesilaus II) were stationed as commanders on the wings: Cleombrotus on the right, Archidamus on the left. This mirrors the Spartan line at earlier battles such as Mantinea, where the Spartans had units on the left and right wings and their allies between (Thucydides 5.67.1). All the men knew their duty and had a long tradition of discipline and following

This sculpture of a fallen warrior from the Greek Temple of Aphaia at Aegina, dating to the 5th century BC, actually shows how difficult it was to lose your shield. The many traditions around Spartan warriors not relinquishing their shields were tied to the idea of not fleeing from battle, yet fleeing was something they did at both Tegyra and Leuctra. (Photo by CM Dixon/Print Collector/ Getty Images)

orders. Unfortunately, Diodorus here explicitly contradicts Xenophon, who states that Archidamus marched out of Sparta only after Leuctra (*Hellenica* 6.4.18). One must simply choose whom to believe, although it seems Xenophon is shielding Archidamus from any blame in the defeat. If present, Archidamus survived the battle, and so must have been one of the principals who accepted the defeat and sent a herald to the Thebans to seek a truce (6.4.15).

In the Spartan army each *mora* was commanded by a polemarch and each unit below the *mora* was commanded by an officer. It seems that each *lochos* was commanded by a *lochagos* (pl. *lochagoi*); the *pentekostys* by a *pentekoster* (pl. *pentekosteres*) and the *enomotia* by an *enomotarchos* (pl. *enomotarchai*). A complication is that Xenophon does mention polemarchs and *pentekosteres* in his history (*Hellenica* 3.5.22, 4.5.7) but does not mention *lochagoi* or *enomotarchai*, even though the *lochagos* would have outranked the *pentekoster*. However, Xenophon does mention *lochagoi* in non-Spartan armies (*Hellenica* 3.1.28, 3.2.16, 4.1.26, 6.2.18; *Anabasis* 3.4.21–22) and he refers to them in his *Spartan Constitution* (11.4). The wider Peloponnesian army probably mirrored the organization we are given for Spartan armies (although usually units outside the Spartans themselves are dealt with only in the vaguest terms). The contribution of light-armed troops, and figures like the state slaves at Sparta (Helots), are often not mentioned at all.

We know several Spartan polemarchs and Archidamus survived Leuctra, for it was they who decided to accept the loss (*Hellenica* 6.4.15). We do find several other magistrates mentioned. One, Prothus, is only mentioned once (*Hellenica* 6.4.2); before the invasion of Boeotia he advised that Cleombrotus should disband his army, and he may have been a polemarch. Others play a slightly larger part. Plutarch mentions Cleonymus, the son of Sphodrias (*Agesilaus* 28.5), and he is also mentioned by Xenophon (*Hellenica* 6.4.14), who tells us that he, Deinon (a polemarch) and Sphodrias himself (one of the king's ten companions) were all killed at Leuctra. Sphodrias had been the governor at Thespiae, appointed by Cleombrotus (*Hellenica* 5.4.15).

This is the Antikythera Ephebe, a 4th-century BC bronze found in 1900 and now in the National Archaeological Museum of Athens (Inv. 13396). The identity of the subject of this sculpture, made in the Peloponnese around 350 BC, is unknown. No known portrait exists of either Epaminondas or Pelopidas. (Leemage/Getty Images)

### Theban commanders

In contrast to the Spartan army, we know much more about the senior officers of the Theban army. We know the overall commander, the Boeotarch **Epaminondas**, and the *lochagos* of the Sacred Band (*Heiros Lochos*), **Pelopidas**. Thanks to Pausanias (9.13.6–7), we also know the names of the other six Boeotarchs present (Malgis and Xenocrates, who supported fighting; Damocleidas, Damophilus and Simangelus who did not; and Brachyllides, who came later and supported Epaminondas). We know nothing else about the command of the Theban and Boeotian armies, although we may be able to suggest some additional detail. Diodorus tells us (15.52.1) that the six Boeotarchs were advisors to Epaminondas. Where

A fragment of a cavalry frieze from the Tomb of Pericles now in the Antalya Archaeological Museum, Turkey. We can see cavalry in *petasos* hat (left), Phrygian helmet (second from right) and Persian headgear (right). It is possible this variety of cavalry represents a mercenary force. (Ad Meskens/Wikimedia Commons, CC BY-SA 3.0)

the others came from were as follows: traditionally, Thebes provided four (two from the city and two from the subject and closely allied cities), Orchomenus and Hysiae two, Tanagra one and then one each from groups of three cities: Akraiphino, Copae and Chaeronea in one group, and Haliartus, Lebadea and Coronea in the other. We do not know precisely where the other six named Boeotarchs came from in Boeotia. It might be worth speculating, however, that the three who supported fighting were from Thebes or the districts under Thebes' direct control. This is further supported by the grave marker from Thebes of the fallen at Leuctra, which records the name Xenocrates (Rhodes and Osborne 2003, pp. 150–51). If this was the Boeotarch, it might suggest he was from Thebes (the grave inscription's final line reads 'nor did we run second to Epaminondas'). We know that one of the seven Boeotarchs was local to Thespiae with troops from that district, and that they were reluctant to fight (Pausanias 9.13.8), so one of Damocleidas, Damophilus or Simangelus was probably from Thespiae. We might suggest that the seventh Boeotarch, Brachyllides, who had been guarding the Mt Cithaeron pass (Pausanias 9.13.7), was perhaps with troops from that district (Plataea, Scolos, Erythrae, and Scaphae), but also one controlled by Thebes. This is attractive since he sided with Epaminondas. If we accept that the Theban phalanx consisted of 4,000 hoplites (the full Theban contingent), perhaps all those in favour of battle were from Thebes or the districts it controlled. The situation may be more complicated, however, as we shall see.

We have some additional information. The grave slab of Xenocrates records the names of three casualties of the battle: Xenocrates, Theopompus and Mnasilaus. We know of no role for the latter two. We also have another veteran, Asopichus, who had run extraordinary dangers at Leuctra and later had the victory monument depicted on his shield (Athenaeus *Deipnosophistae* 13.605a, referring to a work by Theopompus, and Plutarch *The Dialogue on Love/Moralia* 761D). This shield was later dedicated at Delphi. Asopichus, by running such dangers, might be thought to have been a member of the Sacred Band, but the three casualties claimed they had run with Epaminondas as well. Plutarch also tells us that Asopichus was the beloved of Epaminondas, which raises the Sacred Band and Epaminondas.

The non-survival of Plutarch's life of Epaminondas is one of the great tragedies of ancient military history and literature. Nonetheless, we have a rich tradition of material on Epaminondas from a wide range of authors. Xenophon's deliberate marginalizing of Epaminondas' role can easily be seen for what it is when we examine the remainder of that material. Cornelius Nepos does give us a brief biography, but it is in the rich anecdotal tradition where Epaminondas' legacy can be glimpsed.

Epaminondas was born into an ancient aristocratic family at Thebes which had become impoverished (Pausanias 9.13.1, Nepos 15.2.1). His poverty was legendary (Plutarch *Pelopidas* 3.2–4, Aelian *Varia Historia* 2.43, 3.17, 5.5, 7.14, 11.9), essentially putting him on a par with the ideal of the impoverished philosopher, the greatest example being Socrates (*c.* 470–399 BC). Epaminondas dedicated himself to the study of what was necessary in warfare (Nepos 15.2.4–5), and although he is absent from the narratives about the Theban overthrow of Spartan control in 378 BC, he appears soon after and dominated Theban politics and warfare thereafter until his death in 362 BC. He had all the qualities of a great commander and was also Thebes' greatest orator. Epaminondas may have been exiled from Thebes prior to 378 BC since we know he was active there in the 380s BC. This exile probably occurred after 382 BC when the Spartans installed a garrison and when figures like Pelopidas were also exiled and took refuge in Athens (Nepos 16.1.1–2.1). Nepos, however (15.10.3, 16.4.1), maintains that Epaminondas did not participate in the re-taking of Thebes because it pitted citizen against citizen and he refused to stain his hands with the blood of his countrymen.

Despite the silence of Xenophon on Epaminondas at Leuctra and in Theban affairs before 362 BC, he is the dominant figure in our three other main accounts. There are a plethora of anecdotes that establish his role as the mastermind behind Theban tactics at Leuctra (such as Aelian *Varia Historia* 4.16). In Polyaenus and Frontinus' stratagem collections, he is among the individuals with the most anecdotes (12 in Frontinus, second only to Alexander the Great among Greek commanders). Both collections record material not found elsewhere, and so they, and Plutarch's treatment of Epaminondas across several works, reveal different aspects. One of the intriguing factors in Epaminondas' preparation for war is the appreciation of wrestling as a skill for hoplites. This idea is controversial for our conceptions of hoplite warfare, but the sources tell us that Epaminondas

In the aftermath of Leuctra, Epaminondas invaded the Peloponnese and refounded the city of Messene in 369 BC as another nail in the coffin of Sparta. Here, one of the towers along the walls is shown. Removing the Messenian Helots – a source of forced labour that Sparta had relied on since the 7th century BC – from Sparta's control did much to damage the latter's power. (DEA/ARCHIVIO J. LANGE/DeAgostini/Getty Images)

concentrated on wrestling as a skill useful in war. Nepos tells us (15.2.5) that he studied wrestling so that he could seize his opponent in battle and contend with him. This idea is repeated elsewhere (Polyaenus 2.3.6, Plutarch *Table Talk* 2.5/*Moralia* 639F–640A, Diodorus 15.39.1) and even emulated later. The great Achaean League commander Philopoemen modelled himself on Epaminondas, down to being a wrestler (Plutarch *Philopoemen* 3.2).

If Epaminondas was the architect of Theban strategy and tactics, then he needed a builder to realize his plans. That man was Pelopidas. Hand in hand with mentions of Epaminondas come those of Pelopidas, the *lochagos* of the Sacred Band at Tegyra and Leuctra and later a Boeotarch himself. Cornelius Nepos (16.4.3) names Pelopidas as one of the two great citizens of Thebes, second only to Epaminondas. Pelopidas, in contrast to his friend and mentor, was one of the wealthiest men in Thebes (Plutarch *Pelopidas* 3.1–4); Plutarch tells us that Pelopidas dedicated himself to the assistance of worthy men. He attached himself to Epaminondas early on, and the two men dedicated themselves to warfare and the state. We know Epaminondas and Pelopidas fought together at the siege of Mantinea in 385 BC. There, Epaminondas saved the wounded Pelopidas' life (Plutarch *Pelopidas* 4.4–5). This led Dio Chrysostom (*Discourse 49 5*) to name Epaminondas as Pelopidas' own beloved, although he is the only source to do so. The idea that Epaminondas and Pelopidas were loved and beloved ties into other ideas about Theban warfare, especially the composition of the Sacred Band (Epaminondas would command the unit after Pelopidas' death). Asopichus, too, adds to this picture, and there were other men mentioned as Epaminondas' beloveds, fighting next to him in battle. One example is Caphisodorus fighting at Mantinea, where he too died; the two were buried together (Plutarch *The Dialogue on Love*/*Moralia* 761D). Another protégé of Epaminondas was Pammenes, who took command of the Sacred Band following Epaminondas' death at the Battle of Mantinea in 362 BC, commanding it until at least 351 BC (Plutarch *Pelopidas* 18.2). These men may have been senior Thebans and were probably present at Leuctra.

A cast of a scene from the frieze of the *Amazonomachy* from the Mausoleum at Halicarnassus, Caria (modern Bodrum, Turkey). The original is now in the British Museum, and this cast is held in the Athens War Museum. The equipment of the Greeks is contemporary to the building on the monument (*c.* 353–350 BC) and we see *aspis* shields and *dory* spears as well as a *kopis* sword, and details of crests and cloaks. All the male warriors are heroically naked. Other scenes from the frieze show that the *porpax* and *antilabe* grips of the *aspis* shields remained unchanged into the late 350s BC. (Ad Meskens/Wikimedia Commons, CC BY-SA 4.0)

Pelopidas was one of 12 Theban exiles in Athens who returned to Thebes to take back the city (Nepos 16.2.4–5, *Pelopidas* 8.2), and he played an important part in the restoration of Theban power and prestige. After the successful coup in 379/378 BC, he was elected one of the four Boeotarchs at Thebes (*Pelopidas* 13.1). Plutarch explicitly tells us Pelopidas was not a Boeotarch at Leuctra (*Pelopidas* 23.4). Pelopidas led the Sacred Band at Tegyra and achieved a stunning victory over the Spartans there (Plutarch *Pelopidas* 16–17, Diodorus 15.37). Pelopidas may have devised the ideas evident there, of charging his force at a chosen point and targeting the enemy commanders on the right, but it is equally likely that these ideas had been discussed at length by him and Epaminondas, building on Theban history. Tegyra would be the first test of them, and they would be spectacularly repeated at Leuctra where Pelopidas again led the Sacred Band in the front ranks of the Theban phalanx (Plutarch *Pelopidas* 23.2, Nepos 16.4.2).

# OPPOSING FORCES

## *The trouble with numbers*

There are various discrepancies in the numbers deployed by both sides at the Battle of Leuctra. The general consensus has come down to 10,000 Peloponnesian hoplites (including 700 full Spartan citizens, Spartiates) with 1,000 cavalry who faced and fought around 7,000 Boeotians with approximately 700 cavalry. The numbers involved in nearly all ancient battles raise persistent problems for ancient historians and Leuctra is a great test case for this issue. When we are seemingly provided with precise numbers, they can be misleading; light armed troops are usually not mentioned at all in ancient battle accounts and even cavalry can be omitted (as they are in the majority of our sources for Leuctra). The fact we have four (and more) sources for Leuctra does not help us, as they nearly all disagree. What is more, when we are told a precise number of hoplites or the number of men in the phalanx, we often have no idea of the corresponding number of light troops. Often, we must use a known ratio from one of

A Boeotian funerary *stele* dating to *c.* 390 BC and showing *pilos* helmet and cloak. Although there is ample evidence that warriors abandoned a great deal of their armour during the Peloponnesian War and its aftermath, it came back into practical use thereafter. Note the shortness of the Boeotian's *xiphos* sword and the scabbard the warrior carries in his left hand. (Sepia Times/Universal Images Group via Getty Images)

the few occasions when such numbers are mentioned and extrapolate from there. Precise terminology, or the lack of it, can also lead to confusion and can be used inexpertly by authors of a much later age who may not have understood how earlier formations operated. We have examples of both of these at Leuctra. Such precision (of numbers or, indeed, terminology) was not the overriding concern of our sources.

More telling, however, and certainly more evocative is the idea (Diodorus 15.53.2) that as the Boeotians advanced, they suddenly caught sight of the Spartan army covering the entire plain of Leuctra and were surprised by the size of the army opposed to them. This seems unlikely (since the Boeotians will have seen the Spartan phalanx forming as they formed their own), but the idea of a vast, plain-filling enemy is, however, a powerful image – especially when the victor in the battle is outnumbered. Ancient military history is full of vast hosts filling the plain or an uncountable horde (such as Herodotus' Persians). In terms of the participants in the battle, they did not need to know the precise numbers opposing them. At Leuctra, therefore, precise numbers do not really add to the necessary point that the Boeotians were outnumbered and that Epaminondas' choice to offer battle immediately was (eventually) accepted. He knew what he was going to attempt in the battle, and had confidence in his premeditated plan.

None of our sources for Leuctra give us all the numbers involved. Plutarch (*Pelopidas* 20.1) tells us Cleombrotus' force consisted of 2,000 hoplites and 1,000 cavalry. This 2,000 would have been Spartans and equates to almost four full *morai* of the Spartan levy (estimated as about two-thirds of the total number Sparta could field). Using Xenophon (6.4.15, although other sources give higher numbers), only 700 of these were full Spartan citizens. The full Peloponnesian army (with allies) is usually estimated at 10,000 infantry and 1,000 cavalry. By contrast, Polyaenus (2.3.12 and 2.3.14) tells us that Cleombrotus commanded 40,000 men against Epaminondas' 6,000. Yet, the number of 40,000 in Polyaenus is important for an entirely different reason. Frontinus (4.2.6) gives the figures as 3,600 Thebans with only 400 cavalry (so 4,000 in total) against the 24,000 infantry and 1,600 cavalry of the Spartans. It is noteworthy that Frontinus and Polyaenus give the same ratio (6:1) for Peloponnesians versus Thebans, to emphasize their point of a small force facing a numerically superior one. Diodorus tells us (15.52.2) that Epaminondas had conscripted all Thebans of military age and led a force of 6,000 men. Diodorus (15.54.4) also records that Jason arrived from Thessaly with a contingent of 1,500 infantry and 500 cavalry. Xenophon (6.4.20), in contrast, tells that Jason of Pherae was not sent for until after the battle. Pausanias (9.13.3) simply states that Cleombrotus had a force of Lacedaemonians and their allies, and gives no numbers at all. In one regard, we therefore seem to have corroboration between our sources in Diodorus and Polyaenus, usually a good sign, although in this case Polyaenus' high numbers affect credibility.

Following more modern expectations of precise numbers, reconstructions of hoplite, Macedonian phalanx and Roman armies are usually mathematically precise. It also needs to be pointed out that our sources often do have precise, theoretical numbers, when it comes to the mustering of troops – such as the Boeotian League with its 11 Boeotarchs each providing 1,000 men and 100 cavalry, or the ten demes of Athens providing 1,000 men each. Any number of factors could reduce the numbers of men in battle, and radically so.

A similar situation exists with the order of battle in ancient engagements, and Leuctra is no exception. We are sometimes told who occupied the place of honour on the right flank and sometimes the placement of a few other units, but the make-up of the rest of the battle line is unknown or, at best, estimated. We do not know, for instance, where precisely the Sacred Band was positioned at Leuctra and our sources do not offer a clear picture. It has been left to modern accounts to reconstruct that aspect of the battle, and, ironically, their speculations are often as wild as, if not wilder than, the sources they use. The Sacred Band has been placed behind the Theban phalanx, at its forefront, on its extreme left – the list goes on. It is most likely that they formed the front rank of the Theban phalanx, but this is based on the role of Theban elites in earlier battles (Delium and Plataea especially). As we shall see, they may have formed the front two ranks of Epaminondas' heavy column. Modern accounts also go into minutiae (such as the frontage and depth) which may seem relevant and can indeed clarify certain situations, but such aspects are not, on the whole, a concern in our sources – either they considered that the kind of information everyone would be familiar with or it was not regarded as important. My attempts to calculate both Spartan and Theban numbers are used in the hope that they clarify the historical accounts.

As noted above, the numbers for the Spartan army at Leuctra vary. At Tegyra we are told that the Spartans had two *morai* (Plutarch *Pelopidas*

16.1), *c.* 1,200 men, which outnumbered the 500 men of Pelopidas (the Sacred Band at 300 and 200 cavalry, *Pelopidas* 16.2, Diodorus 15.37.1). This is rare detail (although Plutarch does not give a number for the Spartans, and Diodorus tells us they were twice Pelopidas' number (so 1,000 men).

### The Spartans

Spartan male citizens (*homoioi* or equals, also frequently termed Spartiates) were raised by the state to become members of the *agoge* system. This system saw boys raised in barracks from the age of seven, and then from the age of 17 they underwent what is usually described as military training. In Sparta, however, it was seen more as a system that concentrated on those activities devoted to civic freedom (Xenophon, *Spartan Constitution* 7.2). Plutarch characterizes the system (*Lycurgus* 16.6) as being designed to create men who obey commands, endure hardships and conquer in battle. These men made up the core of the Spartan military system (citizens would serve until the age of 60). Supplementing the Spartans themselves were hoplites from other cities in the Spartan homelands of Lacedaemonia, Laconia and elsewhere. These consisted of *Perioeci*, the 'dwellers around' and of allied cities. Thus, we find Peloponnesian armies consisting of many thousands of hoplites, but with a core of Spartan citizens – such as at Leuctra with an army of 10,000 men with only 700 Spartan citizens in it (Xenophon *Hellenica* 6.4.15). The Spartans were seen as the leaders of Greece (Diodorus 15.56.3, Plutarch *Pelopidas* 17.6, Nepos 16.2.4) and excelled all in valour (Herodotus 9.71.1). This view, and the corresponding idea of Spartan invincibility on the battlefield, has recently attracted a great deal of criticism and revision. In the aftermath of Leuctra, however, we can see that the view of Sparta as superior existed in the 4th century BC and one of the obstacles the Thebans had to overcome was to consider themselves equal to their Spartan counterparts.

The Spartan army at the time of Leuctra was organized into six divisions or *morai* and then into smaller units down to the *enomotia*. The actual number of men in each *mora* (and each *enomotia*) is debated by historians, and the ancient sources also disagree on how many men were in each subdivision. Plutarch tells us (*Pelopidas* 17.2) that the *mora* had 500 men (according to Ephorus); according to Callisthenes, 700; and up to 900 according to Polybius and other writers whom Plutarch does not name. A passage where Polybius gives this number for the members of a *mora* does not exist independently.

This *morai* organization was a change from the ancestral organization of the Spartan army into five *lochoi* (Thucydides 5.66.3–68.3), which persisted down to the late 5th century BC. Some time after Leuctra, the Spartan organization seems to have reverted to *lochoi* rather than *morai* (*Hellenica* 7.1.30, 4.20 and 5.10), which further confuses the matter. We have a detailed description of the earlier organization in 418 BC at the Battle of Mantinea (Thucydides 5.66.3–68.3). Later in the Peloponnesian War, in 403 BC, Xenophon mentions the *mora* for the first time (*Hellenica* 2.4.31), a term Thucydides never used. There was probably some kind of reform at Sparta that saw the adoption of the *mora*, although what it was (and when it occurred) is unclear. We can still use Thucydides' account to help untangle Spartan organization at Leuctra.

Xenophon also includes an account of the organization of the Spartan army in his *Spartan Constitution* (11.4). There, and in his continuation of Thucydides' history of the Peloponnesian War, the *Hellenica* (2.4.31), Xenophon introduces the idea that the Spartan army was organized into six *morai*, each commanded by a *polemarchos*, and relates that each *mora* had four *lochagoi*, eight *pentekosteres* and 16 *enomotarchai* (*Constitution* 11.4–10). Therefore, in each *mora* there were four *lochoi*, in each *lochos* two *pentekostyes*, and in each *pentekostys*, two *enomotiai*. Except for the *mora*, this roughly matches Thucydides' earlier descriptions of Spartan organization, although Thucydides has 32 *enomotiai* and fewer *lochoi*. There is an issue with the four *lochoi* in each *mora* (giving a total of 24 *lochoi* across the six *morai*). Later (*Hellenica* 7.4.20 and 5.10), we find 12 *lochoi* mentioned, and it is possible that at the time of Leuctra each *mora* only

Ruins of the Artemision in the ancient Spartan acropolis. Unlike many other Greek cities, Sparta never invested in walls; its hoplites and reputation sufficed. It was only after Leuctra, when Epaminondas invaded the Spartan homeland, that the city was threatened. (PHAS/Getty Images)

Another view of the Spartan acropolis. A further advantage Sparta had over her rivals was that, within the Eurotas River valley, she was protected by mountain ranges on the east and west, the Parnon and Taygetus respectively. Any enemy had to venture a long way south in the Peloponnese to reach Sparta, or Lacedaemon as it was also known, nestled within the Spartan homeland, Lacedaemonia. (DEA/A. GAROZZO/De Agostini via Getty Images)

contained two *lochoi* (Lazenby 1985, p. 8). Xenophon gives us the detail that those serving at Leuctra (and who had been involved in Phocis beforehand) were only men under the age of 55 (*Hellenica* 6.4.17–18).

Xenophon further explains that, when given the order, these *morai* would form abreast, sometimes two, sometimes three, sometimes six in number. At Leuctra, the *enomotiai* formed three men abreast and 12 ranks deep (*Hellenica* 6.4.12) and Xenophon's *enomotiai* therefore have 36 men each (*Hellenica* 6.4.12, 17). This allows us to make the calculation of 72 men in each *pentekostys*; and 144 men in each *lochos*. If we accept Xenophon's number of four *lochoi*, then this gives us a total of 576 men in each *mora*. Most place the *mora* at approximately 600 men, and *Hellenica* 4.5.12 gives a *mora* of 600 men at Lechaeum in 391 BC. The number of *lochoi* is still an issue, but can be solved by taking Thucydides' division of 32 *enomotiai* (four per *pentekostys*) which yields 144 men per *pentekostys*; 288 men per *lochos*; and 576 men per *mora* –which gets us close to the 600 men per *mora* but without the problematic 24 *lochoi*.

### The Thebans

In contrast to Sparta, we are spectacularly uninformed about the organization and training of the Theban army. We do not know its divisions or command structure beyond the highest level, and even there our knowledge does not come from our historical narratives.

This early 4th-century BC grave *stele* from Athens (now in the National Archaeological Museum of Athens (Inv. 3708)) shows a cavalryman riding down his enemy. The scallop out of the fallen man's shield suggests it might be a Boeotian shield, and the enemy, therefore, a Theban. (George E. Koronaios, CC BY-SA 4.0)

The discovery of the major fragments of the *Hellenica Oxyrhynchia* in Egypt between 1906 and 1934 changed our picture, but there are still some issues. Its anonymous author, known as the Oxyrhynchus historian, wrote in the first half of the 4th century BC. The London Papyrus (*P.Oxy.* 842) gives us an account of the constitution of the Boeotian Confederacy, and the author represents a historical tradition independent from both Xenophon and Ephorus.

The *Hellenica Oxyrhynchia* describes a Boeotian Constitution, probably dating from the 5th century BC but which provides a workable framework for the period of Leuctra. It is also possible that the Thebans reinstituted a similar constitution in 378 BC – the leaders (Boeotarchs) certainly use the same titles. The constitution (*Hellenica Oxyrhynchia* 11) divided Boeotia into 11 districts based on population. The districts were comprised of Thebes (two districts) and a further two controlled by Thebes consisting of Plataea, Scolos, Erythrae, Scaphae and other towns; Orchomenus and Hysiae (two districts); Thespiae, Eutresis and Thisbae (two districts); Tanagra (one district); Haliartus, Lebadea and Coronea (one district); and Akraiphino, Copai and Chaeronea (one district). Each district provided a Boeotarch (a military leader, but with other tasks, too) and 60 councillors (*Bouleutai*) for the federal council of 660 members. Each district also provided around 1,000 hoplites and 100 cavalry. Thebes, the largest and most important city in Boeotia, dominated the federation, although the Boeotarchs were theoretically of equal status.

By the time of Leuctra, there were almost as many Thebans as other Boeotians combined (Buck 1994, p. 109), and the League had become a democratic system where all adult male Boeotians voted in an assembly and elected the Boeotarchs. Any Boeotian was eligible to become a Boeotarch, and some non-Thebans were elected. Other committees and officials may have been selected by lot. The office of Boeotarch continued to be a military office. Diodorus calls the new government a league (*synteleia*) (15.38.3, 50.4, 70.2), although citizens were now Boeotians rather than Thespians or Plataeans. To many, this may have seemed like subordination to Thebes, and we find suspicion among some cities in the campaigns, although they are still identified by their localities.

Since each district under its Boeotarch provided 1,000 hoplites and 100 cavalry, and given that there were seven Boeotarchs at Leuctra, this gives modern authors the numbers of 7,000 hoplites and 700 cavalry. At the Battle of Nemea in 394 BC (*Hellenica* 4.2.17), we are told that the Orchomenians (who had revolted from Theban control) were absent and so the Boeotians only brought 5,000 hoplites and 800 cavalry. This suggests smaller numbers than 1,000 hoplites and 100 cavalry per district, in fact almost as few as 550 hoplites per district but close to 100 cavalry (roughly 90). Using these numbers as a calculation for Leuctra, we arrive at fewer than 4,000 hoplites and only 600 cavalry – quite close to Frontinus' numbers. Orchomenus only came back under Theban control after Leuctra so they were absent from the battle. We do not know where the seven Boeotarchs named by Pausanias at

The obverse of the 4th-century BC Theban stater showing the Boeotian shield. No physical evidence of such a shield has been found, although it is depicted on pottery and statuary (usually in a mythological context). It remained a state symbol of Thebes' coinage, suggesting it was a real item. (Photo by Heritage Arts/Heritage Images via Getty Images)

Leuctra (9.13.6) came from or where the other four were with their forces (or even if there were four others – only seven are attested in 372 and 371 BC, see Buck 1994, pp. 108–09 and notes). They may not have been representatives of the original league districts, and those districts may have been redrawn or fallen out of use entirely (although in 378 BC four Boeotarchs were elected, the traditional number of Theban representatives). Presumably, if there were others, they were guarding their cities or perhaps other mountain passes, as Brachyllides was doing before the battle (Pausanias 9.13.7).

We know very little of the structure of the Theban army other than the 1,000 hoplites and 100 cavalry of each district. Xenophon talks (6.4.13) of the Theban *lochoi* in the charge and the elite Sacred Band was itself a *lochos*, commanded by a *lochagos*. If the commander of the 300-strong Sacred Band was a *lochagos*, we might suggest a similar system to the Spartan one, where a *lochos* had between 144 and 288 men, but we do not know. Theban *lochoi* may have been 300 strong; Athenian armies had *lochoi*, too, but that was the smallest division of the Athenian army (*Athenian Constitution* 61.3, *Hellenica* 1.2.3). We might suggest that the Boeotian army had a smaller *lochoi* subdivision based on Thucydides (7.19.3) when, in 413 BC, 300 Boeotian hoplites were sent to Sicily and three commanders are named, two Thebans and one Thespian, who presumably commanded 100 men each. We know of no other officers in the Theban military structure.

### The elites

At the Battle of Leuctra, remarkably, we have two of the most famous elites in ancient Greek warfare going head to head: the Theban Sacred Band and the Spartan *hippeis*. The Sacred Band had also proved themselves at Tegyra. Both units are misunderstood and perhaps controversial, although we possess more information on them than for the larger armies they were a part of.

The first mention of the Spartan *hippeis* occurs in 479 BC, when they accompanied Themistocles back to Athens (Herodotus 8.124.3). We are often not given an exact number for the *hippeis*, but it numbered between 100 and 300 members. Herodotus (6.56) describes a unit of only one hundred 'picked' Spartans who formed the bodyguard of the king, rather than 300 (the latter number is mentioned later, Xenophon *Spartan Constitution* 4.3, Thucydides 5.72.4). In other places they are named a 'bodyguard' (*doruforoi*) rather than the *hippeis* specifically (Xenophon *Hellenica* 4.5.8). Xenophon, usually considered a vital source of Spartan history, only uses the term *hippeis* once, at the Battle of Leuctra (*Hellenica* 6.4.14). Even when Xenophon describes the choosing of the 300 (*Spartan Constitution* 4.3), he does not use the term *hippeis*, although there he does describe the officers, the *hippagretai*. These officers then chose the remaining members. It is clear from other sources that there was fierce competition for places in this unit (*Spartan Constitution* 4.1–6, Plutarch *Lycurgus* 22.4–5, 25.4). Plutarch (*Lycurgus* 22.4–5) suggested

The Boeotian helmet became associated with cavalry later in the 4th century BC, but may originally have been an infantry helmet as well, especially in Boeotia. This 4th-century BC example, now in the Ashmolean Museum, Oxford, was found in the Tigris River, Iraq, and probably belonged to a cavalryman of Alexander the Great who lost it crossing the river. (Gts-tg, CC BY-SA 4.0)

that victors at crown games were selected as candidates. Their place on the battlefield was to fight around the king (Thucydides 5.72.4). Diodorus calls the unit fighting around Agesilaus in 377/376 BC the *skiritai* (15.32.1), but the *hippeis* are clearly meant. The *skiritai* (from a community close to Sparta who usually made up light-armed troops) were traditionally placed on the Spartan left wing (Thucydides 5.67.1), but they are not mentioned in any account of Leuctra.

A line of eight warriors from the Nereid Monument from Xanthos, Turkey. Here, the hoplites, who are all carrying *aspis* shields, are interspersed with lighter-armed troops, two in just tunics and two (without *aspides*) wearing *linothorax* armour. As in other scenes from the monument, several types of helmet are in evidence. (Universal History Archive/ Universal Images Group via Getty Images)

The Theban Sacred Band had a prestigious existence from its formation (around 378 BC) until it was wiped out to a man at the Battle of Chaeronea in 338 BC (Plutarch *Pelopidas* 18.5). According to our sources (Plutarch *Pelopidas* 18–19, 23; Polyaenus *Strategemata* 2.4.1) the Sacred Band was founded by Gorgidas (a figure who soon disappears from the narrative of Thebes' history in 378 or 377 BC). Other origin stories credit Epaminondas with its formation, but these seem unlikely (Dio Chrysostom *Discourse 22: On Peace and War* 3; Hieronymus of Rhodes, in Athenaeus *Deipnosophistae* 13.602a). The Sacred Band was a permanent force equipped and maintained by the city and based in the Cadmea, Thebes' citadel. We do not know how its members were selected or by whom. They were vital in Thebes' rise to military dominance, playing significant roles in her defeats of Spartan forces at the battles of Tegyra (375 BC) and Leuctra (371 BC). The origins of this unit are, however, complicated and controversial. There had been elite units of 300 hoplites earlier in Thebes' history, and the Sacred Band may therefore have been a reconstitution of the Theban 300s which stretched back as far as the Battle of Plataea in 479 BC at least.

Another aspect of the Sacred Band was that it was made up of 150 pairs of homosexual lovers, built on the tradition of an older lover (*erastes*) and a younger beloved (*eromenos*). This unit seems to have attracted comment from Plato (*Symposium* 178E–179A), who claimed that with a small band of lovers fighting side by side, you could conquer the world. This tradition has been challenged (Leitao 2002), but the fact remains that there was a Theban elite unit of 300 hoplites who performed remarkable deeds on the

This Theban grave *stele* from the very late 5th century BC shows a bearded man and beardless youth perhaps reflecting an *erastes*/*eromenos* (lover/beloved) relationship. The youth holds an *aryballos*, a small pottery flask containing oil or perfume, often associated with athletics and wrestling. Various cities encouraged their youths to practise wrestling, and, at Thebes, it may have had a particular association with the Sacred Band. (Universal History Archive/Universal Images Group via Getty Images)

This 4th-century BC fresco from the Macedonian Tomb of Judgement from Mieza (modern Lefkadia, Imathia, Greece) shows *linothorax* armour and *pteruges*. Even though such armour seems to have been optional in the latter part of the 5th century and beginning of the 4th century BC, it came back into use in the 4th century BC, implying that it never fell out of use entirely. (Public Domain)

battlefield. Xenophon makes no mention of the Theban Sacred Band in any of his writings. He does have a passage in his own *Symposium* (8.34) where he challenges the idea of lovers fighting next to one another, as they did at Thebes and Elis, calling it reprehensible. This may have been a challenge to Plato's work as much as a comment on his silence regarding the Sacred Band.

Herodotus talks (9.67) of an elite unit of 300 Thebans, the 'first and best' (*protoi kai aristoi*), who fought on the Persian side at Plataea in 479 BC (the stain on Thebes' reputation). The 'first and best' suggests that they usually fought in the front ranks of a larger Theban army. This unit of 300 was slain to a man by the Athenians, but their brief mention in the context of 479 BC nonetheless raises their existence. They may have been reinstituted after Plataea until the Battle of Oenophyta in 457 BC when Athens conquered Boeotia. The Theban poet Pindar may be referring to these elites in two of his Isthmian poems: *Isthmian 4*, dating to 478 BC, refers to Plataea, and *Isthmian 7* refers to a man dying in the front ranks and is dated probably to after the defeat at Oenophyta in 457 BC.

The elite Theban unit of 300 may have been reconstituted again after Boeotia threw off the yoke of Athens in 446 BC. We next hear of an elite Theban (technically Boeotian) unit

at the Battle of Delium in 424 BC, where Diodorus tells us (12.70.1) that the Boeotians had an elite unit of 300 'charioteers and footmen' (*eniochoi kai parabatai*). This force made up the front line of the Boeotian force. The depth of the Theban formation at Delium was said to be 25 shields (Thucydides 4.93.4) and, with a frontage of 300 men, this would give a total force of 7,500 men. The total number of Boeotians according to Thucydides was 7,000 (4.93.3), and so the detail of the elite unit of 300 providing a front rank is not as far-fetched as it might seem. The evidence from the intervening period hangs on Pindar, but it seems plausible that between 479 and 424 BC, Thebes, or the Boeotian cities more widely, had a unit which was comprised of 300 of their best men and that these, in the title of 'first and best' and explicitly in Diodorus, fought in the front ranks.

When the Sacred Band was formed in 378 BC, therefore, they may have been the reconstituting of a long-standing Theban elite, which used several different names throughout its history. Plutarch tells us (*Pelopidas* 19.3–4) that Gorgidas, the first *lochagos*, distributed the unit among the front ranks of the whole phalanx, but that Pelopidas, after the Battle of Tegyra, kept them together from that point on and treated them as a unit, placing them in the forefront of the greatest conflicts. Pelopidas would command the unit at both Tegyra and Leuctra, until his death in 364 BC, whereupon Epaminondas took command.

*A variety of troop types from the Nereid Monument in Xanthos, Turkey (now in the British Museum). We see an archer (second from left) and several hoplites wearing* linothorax *armour. Even though the shield curtain (the ancient name is unknown but could be* stromata *or* laiseion*) had fallen out of use in Greece by the 430s BC, it may have remained in use in Anatolia; greaves, which fell out of use at around the same time in mainland Greece, are absent on these hoplites. Note that the shield at the far right appears to be slightly smaller in diameter than the other two in the scene. (Prisma/Universal Images Group via Getty Images)*

## Oliganthropia

A further issue must be briefly raised. One of the reasons often given in the ancient sources for the decline in Spartan power was the inability to replace lost manpower – *oliganthropia* (Aristotle *Politics* 1270A33–34). This is evident during the course of the 5th and 4th centuries BC, and the defeat at Leuctra exacerbates the issue. At Plataea in 479 BC, Sparta had 5,000 Spartan citizen hoplites (Herodotus 9.28.2), but at Mantinea in 418 BC that number had shrunk to only 4,200, perhaps as few as 3,600. By the time of the Battle of Coronea in 394 BC, this had slipped further to 2,500 men, and at Leuctra in 371 BC, Sparta could field only 1,500 citizen hoplites. The losses at Leuctra – even if Xenophon's low estimate of 400 Spartiates killed is correct (6.4.15) – was a massive blow. *Oliganthropia* was the one great weakness of the Spartan system.

# OPPOSING PLANS

## Spartan plans

Cleombrotus' signal success in the Leuctra campaign was his stealing a march to the battle by unexpected routes. He had taken the pass via Mt Cithaeron to Plataea in 378 BC (*Hellenica* 5.4.14) and again in 376 BC (5.4.59); it was probably suspected he would take the likeliest pass again in 371 BC, and it was guarded. The Thebans and Athenians had repulsed him easily in 376 BC. Before Leuctra, however, he was at Coronea (Diodorus 15.52.1) and he marched from Phocis into Boeotia (6.4.3), not where expected (the pass to Coronea which was guarded; Diodorus 15.52.7), but to Thisbae and then to Creusis by a mountainous and unexpected route (6.4.4). Cleombrotus then marched up to Leuctra, where the Boeotians had no choice but to face him. The Thebans had been isolated and if they did not fight, the Spartans could remove cities from the confederacy; Diodorus tells us they expected an easy campaign (15.51.4).

Unlike at Nemea in 394 BC (where Aristodemus had commanded the Spartans), there does not seem to have been any real plan by the Spartans to outflank the numerically inferior Boeotians. At Nemea, Aristodemus led his men to the right so they outflanked the Athenians and wheeled around them in order to defeat them fully (*Hellenica* 4.2.19–23). Only in Plutarch's account of Leuctra (*Pelopidas* 23.1–3) is there a suggestion that this was contemplated or attempted by the Spartans, but the order was either

This 4th-century BC Attic red figure vase (now in the Archaeological Museum, Naples) shows an *Amazonomachy*. This scene includes a cavalryman who is armed and armoured in a contemporary manner, wearing a *petasos* hat, cloak and sword on baldric, and who thrusts or throws a spear at his Amazon enemy (who carries a Boeotian shield). (DeAgostini/Getty Images)

# The approach to Leuctra, 371 BC

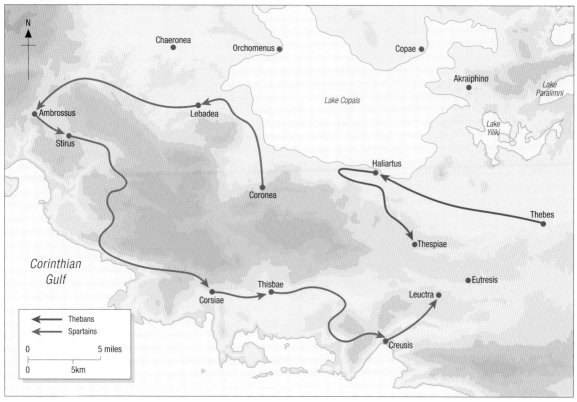

countermanded or not carried out, leading to confusion in the Spartan ranks, and they had not moved position when the Thebans struck. In any case, no manoeuvre was achieved, and this seems like an attempt by Plutarch to explain the Spartan defeat (he is the only source to suggest such a tactic was contemplated).

Rather, in keeping with the conservative Spartan tradition where their reputation should overawe their opponents – such as at Mantinea in 418 BC (Thucydides 5.72.4) or Nemea where, according to Xenophon (*Hellenica* 4.2.18), the Boeotians were too timid to attack the Spartans – the Spartans were to advance against the enemy phalanx. They did this in almost complete silence, accompanied only by *aulos* flutes (Thucydides 5.70.1, Plutarch *Lycurgus* 22.2–3). This disconcerting and unnerving aspect to their advance was in contrast to most other armies, who whooped in excitement (Thucydides 4.34.2). The crescent formation (Diodorus 15.55.3) seems to have come about through the inaction of the Peloponnesian allies in the centre of the line. This was either through disloyalty, unreliability or, more likely, they had become fouled with the retreating Spartan cavalry, although no source other than Xenophon mentions a cavalry action. The crescent therefore was not a tactic, but came about as a result of the two wings advancing but not the centre.

At the same time, there does seem to have been some concession to the fact that the Spartans were facing a dense Theban phalanx. The Spartans therefore drew up their phalanx 12 ranks deep (*Hellenica* 6.4.12). When the Athenians faced the Thebans 25 shields deep at Delium in 424 BC, they

This 4th-century BC Attic red figure *Amazonomachy* scene shows all manner of interesting details of contemporary warfare. The infantry wear *pilos* helmets, hats and cloaks, and they carry *aspides* shields. They wear swords on baldrics but are otherwise unarmoured. One thing to note is how far back some hold their *dory* spears, very close to the *sauroter* (the spike at the rear end of the spear). We also see *xiphos* swords in action. The cavalryman, by contrast, wears a Corinthian helmet and a muscled cuirass and greaves – but his spear seems to be the same as the one used by the infantrymen, rather than a throwing spear or longer cavalry lance. (DEA/A. DAGLI ORTI/De Agostini via Getty Images)

only drew up their line eight deep (Thucydides 4.94.1). At Mantinea in 418 BC, where they had more men, the Spartans only drew up at an average of eight ranks deep (Thucydides 5.68.3).

### Theban plans

At Leuctra, it is likely that lessons from recent battles were observed, absorbed and put into practice by Epaminondas and the Thebans. These can be seen in the deep phalanx, targeting the enemy (especially Spartan) commanders, the elite front rank and the decision by Epaminondas to draw up his line in echelon so that his left wing would avoid coming into contact with the Spartan right.

At the Battle of Delium in 424 BC, the Thebans were on the right of the Boeotian line (Thucydides 4.93.4) and drawn up 25 shields deep. At the Battle of Nemea in 494 BC (where the Boeotians again held the right wing), they had also drawn up their force of 5,000 hoplites in an 'exceedingly deep' formation (Xenophon *Hellenica* 4.218). The alliance of Boeotia, Athens, Corinth and Argos seems to have agreed on a formation 16 ranks deep (which was itself deeper than the usual depth of eight ranks) and the Thebans made their formation deeper still. Xenophon gives no number for the depth. There was a shuffling of places in the alliance battle line prior to Nemea as the Boeotians had held the left at some point facing the Spartans. Xenophon claims the Boeotians refused battle because they faced the Spartans, and the Boeotians eventually swapped places with the Athenian contingent, who faced the Spartans in the battle itself (and were bested). At Nemea, the Boeotians ended up on the right, although it is unclear why the alliance forces swapped positions. What limited evidence we have of depths for hoplite phalanxes reinforces that 16, and indeed 25 ranks, were unusually deep. For a depth of eight we have explicitly Thucydides (4.94.1, 6.67.1) and *Hellenica* (2.4.34). A depth of ten occurs once (*Hellenica* 2.4.11–12); 12 once (at Leuctra, Xenophon *Hellenica* 6.4.12), and 16 twice, at Nemea and in Sicily (Thucydides 6.67.2). We have depths of 50 at Leuctra (*Hellenica* 6.4.12). In the closing year of the Second Peloponnesian War, an Athenian and Spartan formation not less than 50 shields deep faced, and was defeated by, an Athenian rebel formation ten ranks deep (*Hellenica* 2.4.11–12). The Spartans, therefore, were probably confident that their 12-deep formation at Leuctra could account for the depth of the Thebans.

At the Battle of Haliartus in 395 BC, the Thebans inside the city had burst out just as Lysander came up to the walls (*Hellenica* 3.5.19) and seem to have targeted him deliberately. When he fell with his soothsayer and companions, the other Spartans fled in disarray. At Tegyra, too, Plutarch is explicit that the first point of contact and therefore where Pelopidas aimed his charge was on the Spartan right, where the commanders, Gorgoleon and Theopompus, were stationed (*Pelopidas* 17.3).

When it comes to the position of the elite Boeotian or Theban units, we have seen that they occupied the front ranks of the formation at Delium (12.70.1), and probably also at Plataea (Herodotus 9.67) and Oenophyta (Pindar *Isthmian* 7, lines 34–36). Pelopidas placed them in the van at Tegyra (although this may already have been a test of what was to follow at Leuctra – *Pelopidas* 17.2).

All of these lessons were synthesized by Epaminondas at Leuctra: the formation would be deep, probably at least 25 shields deep, as it had been at Delium (Thucydides 4.93.4), although Xenophon gives us a depth of 50 ranks (bolstered by camp-followers and baggage handlers). Other sources talk of the dense column (Diodorus 15.55.4, 56.1; Plutarch *Pelopidas* 23.1) without giving a precise depth, and at Nemea Xenophon, too, talked of the exceedingly deep Boeotian formation without giving an exact depth (*Hellenica* 4.2.18).

The Sacred Band would occupy the front rank just as the Theban and Boeotian elites of the past had at Delium and Tegyra, perhaps at Plataea and Oenophyta, and they would lead the remainder of the Thebans in their initial charge.

This deep Theban formation would be drawn up on the left of the Boeotian line, facing the Spartan right, where the king and other senior magistrates would be stationed. And the first charge would be delivered as it had been at Tegyra, Haliartus and Coronea (*Hellenica* 4.3.17) – at a run. Its first target would be Cleombrotus and the elite men with him, the *hippeis*, other magistrates and senior Spartans. The overwhelming evidence from the traditions that surround his name is that Epaminondas was responsible for the plan and put it into effect with Pelopidas leading the way. Only Xenophon denies this was the case by his silence.

What was new, however, was Epaminondas' idea of drawing up the remainder of the Boeotian forces in echelon, obliquely away from the Theban formation. Whether this was because these forces were unreliable (Pausanias 9.13.9) or weaker (Diodorus 15.55.1) is moot. At the Battle of Delium, the Thebans had won their part of the battle only for the left wing (manned by the Thespians, Tanagraeans and Orchomenians) to be bested by the Athenians (Thucydides 4.96.3). At Nemea, too, the Boeotians were victorious (*Hellenica* 4.2.22), but the Athenians on the left facing the Spartans were defeated (4.2.21). Epaminondas may have seen a way to avoid a similar battle of two halves occurring at Leuctra, and his way of ensuring that the battle would be fought at the place of his choosing, by the troops of his choice, and in the manner he wanted was to have one wing not engage in the fight.

If the additional Boeotian forces to the right of the Thebans were instructed to withdraw from the enemy's advance (Diodorus 15.55.1), they must have been relied upon to do that rather than break and run. The explanations of the troops and non-combatants leaving and coming back reluctantly to the Boeotian ranks in Xenophon (*Hellenica* 6.4.9), Pausanias (9.13.8) and even Polyaenus (2.3.3) seem to be attempts to understand what happened, and who packed the Theban ranks, but they do not make account for the vital role that the additional troops had to play. Had those forces broken and fled, or charged, the Theban contingent could have been surrounded and destroyed (and the Spartan tactics at Nemea showed that Spartan armies were still capable of such manoeuvres).

This hoplite from the Nereid Monument peers over his *aspis* shield and wears *linothorax* armour over a tunic, cloak and an Attic helmet. His underarm spear or sword pose suggests a defensive posture rather than an attacking one. (Prisma/ Universal Images Group via Getty Images)

This 4th-century BC Etruscan fresco (now in the Archaeological Museum, Florence) shows a 'Greek influence' hoplite. The vibrant colours and detail show the *linothorax* armour and the interior bowl of the shield helmet in a striking way. The hoplites of Thebes and Sparta would have been equipped in a remarkably similar fashion. (Photo by CM Dixon/Heritage Images/Getty Images)

More recently, others have wanted to see the cavalry action as the innovation at Leuctra (but no ancient source, with the exception of Xenophon, saw the battle that way). Sherman (note to his translation of Diodorus 15.56.3) wanted to see the real innovation of the Theban cavalry coordinating their charge with the charge of the Theban elite – this conflates the ancient sources in a way they were never combined. The overwhelming ancient tradition is that Epaminondas' tactics at Leuctra were devastating, they were deliberate, and they were to do solely with the phalanx.

# SOURCES

The Battle of Leuctra is one of the most remarkable battles in the entire ancient world. Not just in terms of its impact, innovation or the tactical genius of Epaminondas, but also in terms of the information available to us. We have four surviving accounts of the battle (Diodorus 15.55–56; Plutarch *Pelopidas* 23; Xenophon *Hellenica* 6.4.4–15; and Pausanias 9.13.6–12), more than for any other major engagement in the ancient world. Unfortunately, these multiple sources do more to cloud the truth than reveal it.

Leuctra has also had (almost) more modern reconstructions and analysis by scholars through the centuries than any other battle. These include Anderson (1970, pp. 192–220); Buckler (1980, pp. 46–69); Tuplin (1987, pp. 72–107); Hanson (1988, pp. 190–207); and Konijnendijk (2013, pp. 26–33). Most of these reconstructions have been necessitated by the problems with our sources and, of course, the importance of the battle both in terms of the destruction of the power of Sparta, the rise of Thebes and the watershed it represents in tactical thinking. The differences in these reconstructions can also be attributed to the weight placed on one or another source. At the United States Military Academy, West Point, in the History of Military Art course, the battle is still held up as an exemplary application of the principles of warfare: 'No finer illustration of the successful application of the principles of Mass and Economy of Force is to be found in ancient

# Three interpretations of Leuctra, 371 BC

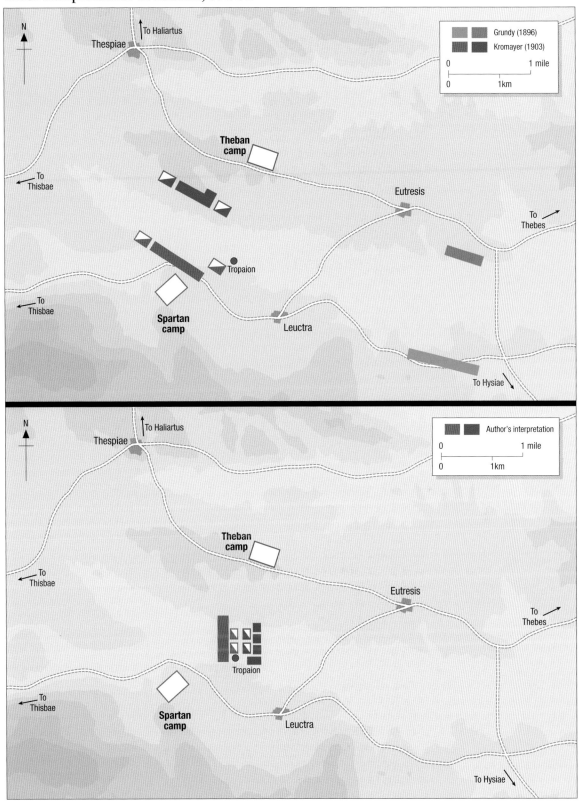

Grundy (1896)
Kromayer (1903)

0         1 mile
0    1km

N

To Haliartus
Thespiae
To Thisbae
Theban camp
Eutresis
To Thebes
Tropaion
To Thisbae
Spartan camp
Leuctra
To Hysiae

Author's interpretation

0         1 mile
0    1km

N

To Haliartus
Thespiae
To Thisbae
Theban camp
Eutresis
To Thebes
Tropaion
To Thisbae
Spartan camp
Leuctra
To Hysiae

This 1774 engraving by K. de Putter of the battle order of Leuctra shows how the battle has been interpreted through time (from *Histoire de Polybe*, Vol. I, Amsterdam, 1774). The deep phalanx, drawn up in echelon, and the refused flank would become tactics emulated again and again. (Icas94/De Agostini Picture Library via Getty Images)

history' (Griess 1984, p. 16). In the field of academia, too, the importance of the battle is seldom underestimated.

Nearly all accounts consider that the battle was something revolutionary, decisive and involved radically innovative tactics introduced by Epaminondas. Hanson, however, argues that 'there were no tactical innovations at Leuctra' (1988, p. 192 n.9) and favours Xenophon's account. This is untrue and favouring Xenophon is misguided. There is a vast tradition across multiple sources that Epaminondas was responsible for tactical innovation at Leuctra and Xenophon's account is highly dissatisfactory in regard to these considerations. Yet, at the same time, Hanson points out that there are disagreements about the role of the Sacred Band, the use of reserves, the use of the oblique attack, the significance of the massed phalanx, the presence of a novel wedge formation and the integration of cavalry and infantry tactics. Notably, these disagreements incorporate several aspects of Xenophon's account whilst at the same time rejecting it because of its anti-Theban and anti-Epaminondas bias. It is only from Xenophon (6.4.12), for instance, that we get the depth of the Theban line as 50 shields deep, any hint of a cavalry action and several other aspects of the battle.

## REPORTING AND INTERPRETING THE OMENS

One important aspect of the build-up to the battle which all our major sources share is an account of the omens (and their various interpretations) which occurred before the battle. Omens, their reporting and interpretation, were vitally important in ancient warfare. It should also be noted that soldiers remain superstitious creatures. Even in our anecdotal sources, omens regarding Leuctra feature prominently. The sources' treatment of these omens also reveals a great deal about their accounts of the battle more generally.

Xenophon (6.4.7) records that the Thebans were encouraged by an oracle who reported that the Lacedaemonians were destined to be defeated at the site of a monument of the virgins who had committed suicide because they

50

had been violated by some Spartans. This monument (the location of which is unknown) was decorated by the Thebans before the battle. News was brought to the Thebans that the temples of the city were opening of their own accord and that this, according to the priestesses, signalled a forthcoming victory. At the shrine to Heracles, the Heracleium, the weapons had disappeared, which was interpreted that Heracles had gone to do battle. Xenophon is sceptical and notes that these may have been rumours put about by the Theban leaders (most probably Epaminondas, whom Xenophon refuses to name). Xenophon nonetheless notes that everything went as foretold for the 'other side', i.e. the Thebans.

Various states used the image of Heracles' club on their coinage. This reverse of a gold quarter-stater was minted by Philip II of Macedon (his son Alexander also used the motif) and cities like Rhodes also used the imagery. At Thebes, with the city's strong connection to Heracles, the club was used as a shield blazon by the Sacred Band and perhaps Thebans more generally (Xenophon *Hellenica* 7.5.20). (DeAgostini/Getty Images)

This account in Xenophon reveals several interesting issues. Firstly, that Xenophon was clearly far more aware of the wider situation following Leuctra than just writing things from the Spartan perspective and his account was clearly not made only from notes of the battle without further, later, reflection. He had certainly learned of the Theban omens prior to the battle. From the anecdotal literature we learn that it was Epaminondas who was credited with causing these omens or, at least, interpreting them when they were reported. Whether Epaminondas' agency in them is true or not is not the point. Ancient military history is full of generals creating or interpreting omens for their advantage. Epaminondas must have been credited with these deeds or interpretations immediately following the battle given its outcome and this must have been the tradition that Xenophon learned. And yet Xenophon refuses to name him; his dismissal with the phrase 'devices of the leaders' appears full of spite.

When we look to Diodorus (15.52.2–7 and 15.53.4–54.4), we get a much fuller account of the omens. He tells us that as the soldiers were marching out from the city, a blind herald met Epaminondas asking him not to take slaves from Thebes but to keep them safe at home. Epaminondas replied with a quote from Homer (*Iliad* 12.243) that the only omen that mattered

This 4th-century BC wall painting from Paestum, a major city in Magna Graecia, southern Italy, shows men duelling with shields. The postures echo others found in Greek pottery and suggest several ways of using spear and shield. The left figure holds his spear close to the base and the right-hand fighter might be argued to represent a left-handed hoplite. (Photo by CM Dixon/Heritage Images/Getty Images)

A frieze of hoplites from the Tomb of Pericles, the ruler of Lycia, dated to 380–360 BC and corresponding exactly to the period of Leuctra. The scene shows a phalanx and all the soldiers are carrying *aspis* shields and wearing a variety of helmets and armour (we can see Illyrian, Phrygian and *pilos* helmets, some with crests, some without). The four front troops clearly wear swords. This remarkable scene (now in the Antalya Archaeological Museum) shows three ranks of hoplites and gives the best sense of the phalanx in surviving art. (Elisa Triolo, CC BY-SA 2.0)

was to fight for 'the land that is ours'. This does perhaps give us a hint that slaves were used as light-armed troops in the battle. A second omen was that the ribbon attached to a man's spear detached in the breeze and wrapped itself around a grave slab. The ease with which events such as this could be reported and interpreted as bad omens makes it seem as if it would be easy to paralyse any activity at all. Diodorus' account also reveals an opposition to not only military action, but also to Epaminondas' leadership. After the second omen, according to Diodorus, Epaminondas led his men out without answer, and Diodorus makes the point that at that moment he was widely criticized. Given the victory he achieved, however, this action was reinterpreted as militarily shrewd.

Later in Diodorus (15.53.4), Epaminondas, who had observed that the omens had unsettled his troops, sought through his own devices to change their minds. He persuaded the men recently arrived from Thebes to say that the weapons at the Temple of Heracles had gone missing, and, word was, that the heroes of old had armed themselves and were coming to aid the Boeotians. This was the same rumour that Xenophon reported, although made into a deliberate stratagem by Epaminondas (something Xenophon is unwilling to credit him with – although it might be a device 'of the leaders').

A second device of Epaminondas' (Diodorus 15.53.4–54.1) was bringing before the troops a man who had come from the Cave of Trophonius who said that the god had directed them, when the Thebans had won at Leuctra, to institute a competition in honour of Zeus. Diodorus has a Spartan exile Leandrias, who was with the Thebans, state that there was a saying amongst the Spartans that they would lose the supremacy of Greece if they were defeated at Leuctra at the hands of the Thebans. And yet more 'oracle-mongers' told Epaminondas of the story of the daughters of Leuctrus and Scedasus who had been raped by Lacedaemonian ambassadors and committed suicide on the plain of the battle – the virgins of Xenophon's account. Further details of this omen are given by Pausanias (9.13.4–6) and

Plutarch (*Pelopidas* 20.3–4). Pausanias adds the names of the daughters (Molpia and Hippo) and the Spartan ambassadors (Phrurarchidas and Parthenius), and that, refused redress at Sparta, Scedasus also committed suicide. According to Pausanias, 'Epaminondas sacrificed with prayers to Scedasus and his girls, implying that the battle would be to avenge them no less than to secure the salvation of Thebes.' Plutarch (*Pelopidas* 20.4–21.4) talks of a dream Pelopidas had about the daughters of Scedasus. The slight differences in these accounts show that they might come from different sources although they are present in some form across all our sources. Diodorus states that the plain was named after Leuctrus and that it was his daughters 'and those of certain Scedasus as well' who were violated, whereas the others do not have this detail – stating instead that the girls came from near Leuctra or were named the Leuctridae. In *On the Malice of Herodotus* 11 (*Moralia* 856F), Plutarch recounts the 'daughters of Leuctrus' version. In Pelopidas' dream, Scedasus demanded a sacrifice, which Pelopidas then mentioned to the seers and commanders. A mare then broke free in camp and provided the required auburn-haired sacrifice. This anecdote falls into the field of the interpretation of omens by commanders, in this case by Pelopidas.

Epaminondas' plan with all these omens (and Diodorus says there were many more) was to rid the Thebans of their superstition so that they would stand ready for battle with 'courage in their hearts'. Frustratingly, Plutarch (*Agesilaus* 28.4) states that he has written of the many omens in his (lost) life of Epaminondas. The anecdotal record also supports the view that there were many more (such as Pausanias 4.32.3–6 on the ancient Messenian king Aristomenus' shield, brought to Leuctra by Xenocrates). Polyaenus (2.3.8) records that Epaminondas got the Thebans to take courage by two tricks. The first is a version of the story in Diodorus regarding Trophonius, although the details in Polyaenus make it clear he followed a different source. The second trick in Polyaenus' stratagem provides more details of Epaminondas' device around the Temple of Heracles. According to Polyaenus, Epaminondas had prearranged with the priest to remove the weapons, clean them and lay them by the god's statue. When the Theban soldiers arrived to pray (encouraged to do so by Epaminondas), they saw the open temple, and the cleaned weapons, ready for war at the feet of the statue. This filled the soldiers with divine courage as if they had Heracles himself as their general.

Again, it is clear that Polyaenus' source must be different from the other versions of this story, not only in the details but also in terms of the timing – occurring before the Thebans set out and therefore suggesting greater predetermination (and religious cynicism) on Epaminondas' part. Another brief version of this anecdote occurs in Frontinus (1.11.16). Polyaenus records another omen at 2.3.12, one not found in the other accounts but which has the same elements. A wooden statue of Athena held a spear in her right hand and had a shield lying in front of her knees. Epaminondas brought a sculptor in the night to make the statue grip the shield in her left hand. When the soldiers saw the altered statue, they proclaimed that Athena herself had taken up arms against the Spartans.

It is in both of these anecdotes that Polyaenus mentions the 6,000 Thebans against the 40,000 Spartans. His emphasis is on how the Thebans were inspired to defeat a numerically superior foe by these omens. Epaminondas'

The hill to the south of the field which may have been the site of the Spartan camp (*Hellenica* 6.4.14). Taken from the position of the Tropaion, this clearly shows there was not much room for manoeuvre on the Spartan right flank (or the Theban left). The flight of the Spartans from the battlefield was clearly difficult, given it had to be made around the victorious Theban left as it turned right into the Spartan allies in the centre. (Myke Cole)

shrewdness and foresight in performing these acts before the departure of the army in Polyaenus seems to reflect a tradition different to those in Diodorus, and Plutarch (and Xenophon). Nonetheless, there, too, the responsibility lies with Epaminondas. Frontinus also records the incident of the ribbon wrapping itself around the grave slab (1.12.5), also found in Diodorus (15.52.5–6), but again it seems to come from a different source since Diodorus has Epaminondas make no reply but simply leads his men out of the city, whereas Frontinus records that Epaminondas replied: 'Do not be concerned, comrades! Destruction is foretold for the Spartans. Tombs are not decorated except for funerals.'

It is impossible that Xenophon did not know of this rich tradition of omens, all of which are attached to Epaminondas. That Xenophon records them at all without the association with Epaminondas is odd indeed, but simply adds to the mistrust in his account. The idea that many of these omens occurred before the army set out can be seen in Plutarch's *Sayings of Kings and Commanders* 8 (*Moralia* 192F–193A), where they begin when the Spartans threatened invasion. There are also several occasions in the sources where Epaminondas either interprets a thunderclap or refuses to let a thunderclap deter his action (Plutarch *Moralia* 192F–193A; Polyaenus 2.3.4; Frontinus 1.12.6 – a meteor).

## THE BATTLE IN BRIEF

Our four sources for the battle will be dealt with in full below, and the various aspects of each discussed as they arise. This method has the disadvantage, however, of only revealing what happened in pieces (and sometimes ill-fitting pieces at that). To counter this, a brief overview of the battle is provided here.

In camp, a debate was held among the Theban leadership. Six Boeotarchs were equally divided between fighting (led by Epaminondas) or withdrawing.

# The Battle of Leuctra, 371 BC

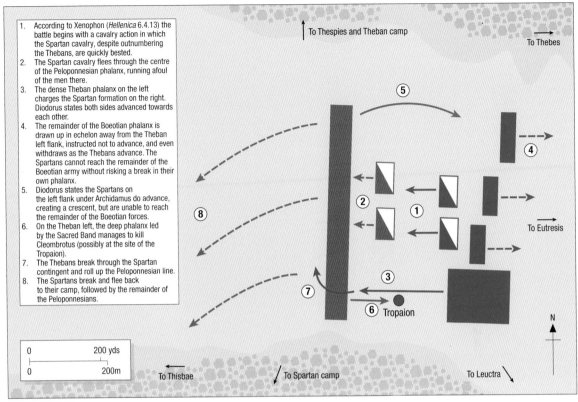

1. According to Xenophon (*Hellenica* 6.4.13) the battle begins with a cavalry action in which the Spartan cavalry, despite outnumbering the Thebans, are quickly bested.
2. The Spartan cavalry flees through the centre of the Peloponnesian phalanx, running afoul of the men there.
3. The dense Theban phalanx on the left charges the Spartan formation on the right. Diodorus states both sides advanced towards each other.
4. The remainder of the Boeotian phalanx is drawn up in echelon away from the Theban left flank, instructed not to advance, and even withdraws as the Thebans advance. The Spartans cannot reach the remainder of the Boeotian army without risking a break in their own phalanx.
5. Diodorus states the Spartans on the left flank under Archidamus do advance, creating a crescent, but are unable to reach the remainder of the Boeotian forces.
6. On the Theban left, the deep phalanx led by the Sacred Band manages to kill Cleombrotus (possibly at the site of the Tropaion).
7. The Thebans break through the Spartan contingent and roll up the Peloponnesian line.
8. The Spartans break and flee back to their camp, followed by the remainder of the Peloponnesians.

To Thespies and Theban camp

To Thebes

To Eutresis

Tropaion

To Thisbae

To Spartan camp

To Leuctra

N

0    200 yds
0    200m

With the arrival of the seventh Boeotarch, who sided with Epaminondas, the decision was taken to fight. The Boeotian camp followers and baggage handlers, as well as some reluctant troops, may have left at this point. These may have been harassed by Spartan light-troops and cavalry, and returned to the ranks before the battle.

On the field at Leuctra, Epaminondas drew up the Boeotian line with the Thebans themselves, in a dense phalanx much deeper than usual, on the left facing the Spartan king, who was, as was traditional, stationed on the Spartan right. The 300 members of the Theban Sacred Band with their commander Pelopidas were also stationed on the left, as the front rank of the Theban formation. The remainder of the Boeotian line was drawn up obliquely or in echelon, that is diagonally away from the massed Theban phalanx on the left. As the Theban left advanced towards the Spartan king, therefore, the remainder of the Boeotian line would not be required to fully engage with the corresponding part of the enemy phalanx, and may have actually withdrawn as the remainder of the Spartans advanced.

The battle would be decided by the densely packed Theban phalanx's clash with the Spartan right, elite versus elite. This is indeed what happened. The Theban phalanx (led by the Sacred Band in front) smashed into the Spartan right wing and, after a time, felled the Spartan king Cleombrotus and much of his *hippeis* bodyguard. The Thebans then turned and began to roll up the Peloponnesian line. The Peloponnesian line broke and fled from the field back to the Spartan camp.

The battlefield of Leuctra looking towards the Tropaion. The Spartan position will have been to the left, with the Thebans advancing from the right. Parallel to the road, an irrigation canal now divides the Tropaion from the remainder of the battlefield which is clearly private farmland (but which remains largely unchanged from photos taken in the 1970s and earlier). This photo is taken from a hill south of the battlefield and another possible location of the Spartan camp. The distance between the Tropaion and the hill does not allow for the manoeuvres suggested by Xenophon. (Myke Cole)

# DIODORUS

Diodorus' account of the battle (15.55–56) gives us a great deal of detail. He begins by telling us that the descendants of Heracles (Cleombrotus and Archidamus) were stationed as commanders on the wings. On the Boeotian side, Epaminondas was in 'an unusual disposition of his own' (15.55.1), selecting the bravest men and placing them on one wing where he would fight with them himself. The weaker troops he placed on the other wing, instructing them to avoid battle by gradually withdrawing as the enemy attacked. He therefore drew up his phalanx in an oblique formation, opting to decide the battle with the wing where the elite were stationed (15.55.2). This could mean the entire Theban contingent (the bravest men) or the Sacred Band (whose stationing we get from other sources). Accepting the Sacred Band as the front rank of the Theban army, this calculation might work. A front rank consisting of the elite for the Theban phalanx, like at Delium (Diodorus 12.70.1), provides too many men (300 x 50 = 15,000). Even if we do not accept Xenophon's Theban phalanx 50 ranks deep (*Hellenica* 6.4.12), and take the depth as per the Battle of Delium at 25 ranks (Thucydides 4.93.4), this number is too high (300 x 25 = 7,500). If we take this depth of 25 and suggest that the Sacred Band provided the front two ranks and the same depth at Delium (150 x 25 = 3,750), this gets us close to the full contingent of 4,000 men taken from the four Theban-controlled districts. In which case, the additional ranks (as suggested by Xenophon, and even if not as many as 50) may have consisted of non-combatants. Perhaps they were also made up of all the men of military age whom Epaminondas conscripted (Diodorus 15.55.2). He may even have recruited slaves (Diodorus 15.52.3). What is more, the idea that the Theban phalanx consisted of all the men available makes Diodorus' assertion that Epaminondas selected the bravest men for his formation on the left wing a criticism of those who did not wish to fight. If this contingent consisted of all the Theban hoplites and those from Theban-controlled districts, and every Theban available, Diodorus (and Epaminondas) praise them for their selection, and they all may well have been considered elite in that regard.

Diodorus (15.55.3) has the battle begin on both sides simultaneously – with trumpets sounding on both sides and each charging, uttering their battle cry. The Spartan attack took on a crescent formation, where each wing moved towards the enemy; but the Boeotian right wing withdrew in the face of this Spartan advance, just as it had been instructed to do. On the Theban left, the troops there engaged in double-quick time, meeting the Spartans in hand-to-hand combat.

Diodorus tells us that the battle was at first evenly poised, but soon (15.55.4) Epaminondas' men derived advantage from their valour and the denseness of their ranks. Many Peloponnesians began to fall, felled by the Theban elite corps. All the Peloponnesians suffered wounds to their fronts (meaning they had not yet turned and fled). As long as Cleombrotus, fighting in the midst of the Spartan right (15.55.5), lived, there were comrades willing to die in his defence, and the battle was evenly poised. The king, however, perished after suffering many wounds, and men thronged around his body, a great pile of corpses building up.

The death of Cleombrotus left the Spartan right wing without a commander (Diodorus 15.56.1). Many of those who should have taken over command fell with him, and Epaminondas led his 'heavy column' and bore down on the Spartans. The sheer force of this assault made the Spartan line buckle, and although the Spartans got possession of the body of Cleombrotus, they were not strong enough to achieve victory. The Theban elite outdid them in feats of courage, and Epaminondas exhorted them within the ranks (15.56.2). The Lacedaemonians were forced back at first, but stayed in formation; however, with many falling and no commander, they turned and fled in complete rout. Epaminondas' corps pursued them and

Looking across the modern irrigation canal at the battlefield of Leuctra; a slight hill on the right may have been the Theban camp, although it may also have been further to the east if the Spartans camped at Leuctra itself. The field gives the sense of Boeotia's fields being ideal ground for hoplite warfare, although the slight downhill right to left may have aided the Thebans. (Myke Cole)

achieved a great victory (15.56.3). Diodorus credits the victory most of all to Epaminondas' shrewdness, overcoming the 'invincible leaders of Greece'. Diodorus records (15.56.4) that more than 4,000 Lacedaemonians fell, but only 300 Boeotians.

### Analysis

Diodorus seems to present a convincing picture of the battle, yet there are issues. He does not mention cavalry at all; he does not explicitly name the Sacred Band (although he refers to a Theban elite); and he only makes passing reference to the heavy column and dense formation of the Thebans. It is clear from Diodorus, however, that Epaminondas' tactics at Leuctra were both deliberate and premeditated. We know that Diodorus was using Ephorus as a source (15.60.5), as well as several other authors (16.14.3). Assuming Diodorus did use Ephorus for his account, we can put Polybius' criticisms of Ephorus (12.25f.1–7, regarding both Leuctra, and Mantinea in 362 BC) to the test.

Polybius, probably writing after 150 BC in Rome, states that, to him, Ephorus had some idea of naval warfare but that he was entirely in the dark when it came to land battles. When Ephorus described the battles of Leuctra and Mantinea, his account provoked laughter because he seemed perfectly inexperienced in such things and had never seen a battle. Most of Polybius' criticism, however, seems aimed at Ephorus' account of Mantinea, since Polybius admits Leuctra was a simple affair where only one part of the army was engaged and Ephorus' ignorance is therefore not conspicuous. In his account of the Mantinea, however, Polybius accuses Ephorus of creating an imaginary description and that the battle was not understood by the writer.

Unfortunately, Ephorus' account of the battle does not survive directly, so we cannot compare it with what Polybius wrote. We can, however, compare it with Diodorus' account (15.54–56), which, in all probability, was based on Ephorus' account plus other sources (including the Oxyrhynchus historian). We should note, however, that Polybius does not say that Ephorus' account of Leuctra was mistaken or incorrect. Rather, because it was a 'simple affair', Ephorus' account conceals his ignorance of land-based military matters. The problem arises that the other surviving accounts do not seem simple at all.

Another anecdote regarding Ephorus is also worth recalling. In *Moralia* 514 C, *Concerning Talkativeness*, Plutarch gives an account of a native of Chaeronea (Plutarch's home town) who (in the 2nd century AD) had read Ephorus and would bore everybody to death by narrating Ephorus' account of Leuctra. He gained the nickname 'Epaminondas' (which might suggest that Ephorus, too, gave all credit to Epaminondas). From this, it could be implied that Plutarch had read Ephorus himself and therefore had correctly surmised the source of the dreaded tale. It is also likely that Plutarch had heard the details of Ephorus' account so many times

The reverse side of the Tropaion (taken looking towards the road and possible Spartan camp) clearly showing the extent of the restoration. The dome of nine *aspides* (each 97cm in diameter) measuring 3.65m was all that was left of the original monument (discovered in 1839) when restoration started in 1961. The fragments of *metope* (clearly visible here) allowed the height to be estimated. (Myke Cole)

that when he came to write his own account of Leuctra, which for us only survives in the *Pelopidas* (20–23) and *Agesilaus* 28, he may have relied on this familiarity. In his account of the Battle of Tegyra (*Pelopidas* 17.2), Plutarch tells us that he used Ephorus, Callisthenes and Polybius. We can reasonably expect that the account of the battle in the *Epaminondas* would have been much longer. It is worth noting that Xenophon's *Hellenica* is not mentioned here by Plutarch, even though he was aware of Xenophon.

In summary, Diodorus' account seems to be straight-forward and sensible, and the main aspects of the battle are clear – the Theban line being drawn up in echelon, the massing of one wing with elite troops, the withdrawal of the Theban right wing as the Spartan left advanced, with all of these deliberate and planned by Epaminondas. The defeat of the Spartan right wing, the death of Cleombrotus and the rout that followed are clearly presented. There

are certain aspects of the account which might relate to Polybius' criticisms: the selection of the men to occupy the Theban left wing as described (being the bravest from the entire army) is perhaps misleading, as is the almost accidental mentioning of the densely packed formation of the Theban left pushing the Spartans back. These elements are, however, present, and the sense of what happened is clear. The more risible aspects to the account for Polybius comprise the depiction of Cleombrotus' bravery, the Spartans receiving all their wounds to their fronts, and the fight over the king's body – seeming more in the vein of heroic warfare (although such tropes continued well into the Roman period and beyond).

Another 4th-century BC Etruscan fresco funerary relief showing details of the hoplite panoply (now in the Archaeological Museum, Florence). Italian 'hoplites' are shown in the same equipment as those on mainland Greece (although they are shown in greaves, which dropped out of use in the 5th century BC in Greece). Despite the close similarity of equipment, the idea that Italian armies operated in the same way as Greek hoplite phalanxes has been challenged. (DeAgostini/Getty Images)

The fragments of the Tropaion at Leuctra looking towards the Theban position and possibly their camp (on the slight hill behind the buildings in the middle ground). It is possible the camp was further east if the debate about offering battle is to be followed. Anecdotes about the reluctant not coming out for battle may also have been difficult to accept if they camped close to the battlefield itself. (Myke Cole)

## THE CHARGE OF THE THEBAN PHALANX AT LEUCTRA, 6 JULY 371 BC (PP. 60–61)

Shown here are the Theban Sacred Band (**1**), led by Pelopidas (**2**, just as he had done at the Battle of Tegyra), charging the Spartan phalanx (**3**). The Sacred Band made up the front ranks of the larger Theban phalanx. Sources differ over whether or not the Sacred Band made up the front left corner of the Theban army's front rank, but it seems most likely that it did (based on Tegyra, Delium and other evidence). Each man has the club of Heracles on his shield (**4**) and the superior training of the Sacred Band is shown in their precision and drill. The Thebans as a whole are probably 150 shields wide, but up to 50 ranks deep behind. These additional numbers added their weight to the charge, although it is unclear precisely what this meant. There may have been fewer than 50 ranks of effective hoplites – Xenophon has the rear ranks comprise non-combatants, and the Boeotian phalanx at the Battle of Delium was only 25 ranks deep. Pelopidas is on the right edge of the Sacred Band (from the Theban perspective), while Epaminondas leads the remainder of the Thebans forward.

The Theban ranks of the Sacred Band display a variety of equipment though the club of Heracles is a distinctive unifying feature (it seems regular Theban hoplites also employed the club of Heracles as a shield device). The remainder of the Boeotian army was drawn up in echelon away from the Thebans stationed on the left flank. As the Thebans charged, these units were told to withdraw in the face of any enemy advance.

The Spartans, perhaps as a counter to the Theban depth, have drawn up 12 ranks deep (more than the typical eight ranks of Spartan armies). Both Plutarch and Xenophon give explanations of Spartan disorganization: whether from a failed attempt at manoeuvre or other factors, their discipline was not as sound as that of the Thebans. Nor were they as confident. They would, nonetheless, fight bravely while they could.

Is the straight-forward nature of Diodorus' account tantamount to hiding the ignorance of Ephorus? Perhaps. The account as we have it could mean that Diodorus either did not use Ephorus, or that he has tidied up the account using another source. Another possibility is that Polybius expected more from Ephorus, although we do not know what (superior) source(s) Polybius was using to assess Ephorus or Diodorus; it certainly was not Xenophon. It has even been argued that Xenophon influenced Polybius in other ways (McGing 2010, pp. 62–63). If Polybius was comparing Ephorus with Xenophon's account (and siding with the latter), it would surely not have been a 'simple affair'; the details are so unalike. Indeed, as we shall see, Xenophon and Ephorus seem to be describing almost different battles. The other accounts, Plutarch and Pausanias, can also be allied to Diodorus much more than to Xenophon.

# PLUTARCH

Plutarch's account of the Battle of Leuctra (*Pelopidas* 23) launches straight into the action, and gives more details and different explanations than Diodorus' account. Epaminondas drew up his phalanx obliquely towards the left so that the right wing of the Spartans (from the Theban perspective) would be separated as far as possible from the rest of the Greeks (23.1). Epaminondas aimed to thrust back Cleombrotus by a fierce charge in column with all his men (meaning the Thebans). Plutarch tells us that the Spartans saw what he was doing and began to change their formation, opening their right wing to encircle Epaminondas' left. At this moment (23.2), Pelopidas darted forth from his position and with his band of 300 on the run before Cleombrotus had extended his wing as planned or brought it back to its original position. The Spartans were, therefore, not in formation but moving confusedly when Pelopidas reached them. Plutarch points out (23.3) that the Spartan training should have meant that they were able to fight next to whosoever was beside them. The Theban column therefore bore down upon the Spartans (23.4). Moreover, Pelopidas, leading the Sacred Band, engaged them with incredible speed and boldness, and owing to the skill and courage of his men, the Spartans were confounded. There followed such a flight and slaughter of the Spartans as had never been seen. He tells us that even though Epaminondas was Boeotarch, and Pelopidas only commanded a small portion of the whole force, he nonetheless won as much glory as Epaminondas did.

Certain aspects of Plutarch's account can be reconciled with Diodorus: the drawing up of the line in echelon as a deliberate plan of Epaminondas, and the charge in column (although it is not mentioned as being especially dense). Other aspects of Plutarch seem to add to our knowledge (Pelopidas and the Sacred Band being at the forefront of the charge). At the same

The iron breastplate of Philip II of Macedon from his tomb in Vergina. Philip was a hostage at Thebes between 368 and 365 BC, prior to becoming king in 359 BC, where he may have learned the tactical thinking of men such as Epaminondas and Pelopidas (Justin 6.9.7, 7.5.2, Plutarch *Pelopidas* 26.5). The armour of the Macedonian infantry would remain much the same as during the earlier 4th century BC, but Philip would change to a smaller round shield (the *pelte*) and a longer spear (the *sarissa*) – both trends already apparent earlier in the century. He would also adopt a deep phalanx – usually 16 ranks deep, but it could double to 32 ranks deep. (DEA/G. DAGLI ORTI/De Agostini via Getty Images)

Another view of the Leuctra Tropaion, this one looking almost directly west. If we are right in identifying this as the position of Cleombrotus and the Spartan right, the remainder of the Spartan line will have been drawn up to the right of this image. (Myke Cole)

time, the description of an attempted Spartan manoeuvre to outflank the Thebans seems unreconcilable (and contradicts Diodorus' account that the two sides charged each other). Several of Plutarch's details actually take away from the battle being 'a simple affair' – such as an attempted envelopment that was thwarted by the rapid charge of an elite unit.

Plutarch's details seem to reflect an early tradition (even though he was writing about 450 years after the event) of analysis of the intentions and minute tactics of the battle. The Spartans being caught in mid-manoeuvre could reflect an attempt to explain their devastating defeat (cf. Xenophon later, although the actual explanations differ). This, of course, assumes that the analysis present in Plutarch comes from his source, rather than Plutarch himself. The plethora of anecdotal accounts of Epaminondas and Pelopidas' conduct in the battle certainly reveal that there were many accounts of the battle to draw from, indeed many more than we usually consider. Plutarch's idea that the Spartans were not in formation when Pelopidas' Sacred Band reached them seems unlikely, even though Plutarch (and his source) give a reason for it. The discipline and drill of the Spartans would surely not have permitted such a shambles (again something Plutarch seeks to explain). We should note, however, that the Spartan manoeuvre to outflank had not been achieved (only 'begun' before being countermanded), and so the Thebans will have charged a Spartan phalanx that looked relatively solid and unchanged. It is also highly unlikely, as Hans Delbrück pointed out (1908, p. 167), that 300 Thebans could halt a manoeuvre by a vastly superior force of thousands. This is despite the emphasis in the stratagems of Polyaenus and Frontinus, especially of a small, well-led and highly motivated force achieving amazing results against a vastly superior force. This aspect of the battle appeals to modern theorists especially. What Plutarch's account does provide is a reason why the Spartans were so decisively beaten and why they fled. We might interpret the manoeuvre in Plutarch as an explanation of the increase in depth of the Spartan phalanx to 12 ranks (*Hellenica* 6.4.12) if this was done late in deployment.

On the whole, however, Plutarch's account adds depth of detail to Diodorus' account, and logically makes sense of the battle. There is nothing in Plutarch that contradicts Diodorus. With Plutarch's *Moralia* passage in mind, it may suggest that Diodorus has simplified Ephorus' account and, perhaps, restored some of the 'simple affair' that Polybius referred to.

The oblique formation to the left recorded in Plutarch can be read as a Theban attempt to avoid an outflanking manoeuvre by the Spartan left (there is no mention of the rest of the Spartan formation in Plutarch). They were vastly outnumbered and the echelon formation mitigated that disparity in numbers. It is worth noting that the tendency of the phalanx was a movement to the right (Thucydides 5.71.1) usually explained as the man stationed to the left of his comrade seeking shelter in his friend's shield. This view has been challenged in various reconstructions of Hoplite warfare, and yet the phenomenon of phalanxes moving towards the right was observed and recorded. If Epaminondas deliberately made his phalanx charge straight on or move to its left, this is notable, although it was also the logical and necessary tactic for him to undertake to attack the Spartan right and avoid being outflanked. The action of the Sacred Band led by Pelopidas was intended to block or thwart that Spartan outflanking manoeuvre further, which is what it achieved with spectacular success. Plutarch's alternatives for the result of the Sacred Band's manoeuvre – that it either prevented the Spartan manoeuvre, or that it forced the Spartans back into line – gives some support to Diodorus' account of men thronging.

However, there are still issues with Plutarch's account; again, the cavalry is not mentioned. Nonetheless, in Plutarch as in Diodorus, responsibility for the battle plan lies overwhelmingly with Epaminondas. It is interesting to note the credit accorded to Pelopidas in Plutarch's account. Perhaps this should be expected in a biography of Pelopidas, but it may also reflect the deliberate and premeditated nature of Epaminondas' plan, something Pelopidas was no doubt a part of. As we have seen, at Tegyra (*Pelopidas* 17.3–4) Pelopidas led his men on the left and attacked the Spartan commanders Gorgoleon and Theopompus. The unnamed commander at Haliartus (*Hellenica* 3.5.19–20) could also have provided similar insights; when the Spartan commander Lysander fell, his army fled. No doubt Pelopidas and Epaminondas had conferred and 'compared notes'. We might even recall the anecdote of the snake (Polyaenus *Strategemata* 3.2.15) where Epaminondas, urging the Thebans to attack the Spartans (the exact context is not given, but it was most probably before Leuctra), grabbed a snake and crushed its head, saying that without the head the rest of the body was useless. Theban experience had shown this already. The anecdote is not recorded elsewhere, but suggests

A Scythian short sword sheath from the 4th century BC, found in the Dnepropetrovsk region, Ukraine (now in the Institute of Archaeology of the National Academy of Science of Ukraine, Kiev). This artwork shows how widespread hoplite equipment had become. The shield, helmets and cuirass, as well as the marching with spear butt in the left hand that also holds the shield in place, are all practices we find in mainland Greece. (DEA/A. Dagli Orti/ Getty Images)

The rear of the Leuctra Tropaion looking towards the south-west, the direction from which the Spartans marched to Leuctra. The hill here is further west, but is another candidate for the site of the Spartan camp, perhaps more appealing since the Spartans could flee to it without having to negotiate the victorious Thebans. The nine *aspides* of the dome might represent the men from Boeotia who fought, even though only seven Boeotarchs are named in Pausanias' account. (George E. Koronaios, CC BY-SA 4.0)

both Epaminondas' tactics at Leuctra (in both targeting the Spartans and their commanders) and also the underlying idea of freeing Greece of Spartan domination.

Pelopidas' valuable experience as the commander of the Sacred Band linked into Epaminondas' plan at Leuctra. Cornelius Nepos' summary (16.4.2) makes this clear: although Epaminondas was the commander-in-chief, Pelopidas, as the leader of the select corps, was the first to break the Spartan phalanx.

Plutarch does refer briefly to Leuctra again in the *Agesilaus* (28.5), recording that 1,000 Lacedaemonians fell, including Cleombrotus and Cleonymus, the son of Sphodrias. Cleonymus was struck down three times in front of his king, but rose again each time, before finally being killed by the Thebans. This accords with Diodorus and Xenophon's account of the battle (*Hellenica* 6.4.14), although Xenophon does not recount these details about Cleonymus.

Plutarch records some details of the battle elsewhere, such as the Thebans overcoming the Spartans because they were practiced wrestlers (*Table Talk* 2.5/*Moralia* 639f–640A). Such a view is corroborated by diverse sources (Polyaenus 2.3.6, Nepos 15.2.4–5). The mass grave of the Sacred Band at Chaeronea, erected after they fell to a man there, contained 254 skeletons in seven rows, each of which had a *strigil*, for scraping sweat/oil from the skin – perhaps part of a wrestler's accoutrement. Here Plutarch even goes so far as to justify the idea of the hoplite as wrestler, using passages from (lost works of) Aeschylus and Sophocles. Later, the great Achaean League commander Philopoemen is supposed to have modelled himself on Epaminondas, down to being a wrestler (Plutarch *Philopoemen* 3.2). Plutarch elsewhere (*That Epicurus Actually Makes a Pleasant Life Impossible* 18/*Moralia* 1099E) records that the Thebans, down to his own day, celebrated the victory at Leuctra, just as the Athenians celebrated Marathon. A factor in the significance of Leuctra (questioned by modern authors) is Plutarch's assertion that thereafter, the chief Theban commander was stationed in the left wing of their armies (*Roman Questions* 78/*Moralia* 282E).

The Altikulaç Sarcophagus from Hellespontine Phrygia showing a cavalryman attacking a Greek (mercenary?) *psiloi* or *peltast*, dating to the early 4th century BC. Note the *kopis* sword and two throwing javelins on the left figure, and the smaller round shields (*pelte*) with central hand grip. The sarcophagus is now in the Troy Museum, Turkey. (Elisa Triolo, CC BY-SA 2.0)

# PAUSANIAS

Pausanias' account of Leuctra (9.13.6–11) also states that Epaminondas was the leader and the clear mastermind behind Theban tactics, even though he was one of seven equal-ranking Boeotarchs. Pausanias, like Plutarch, also seems to rationalize the accounts we have. He gives us the names of the seven Boeotarchs, a detail which is not given in any other surviving account.

Pausanias opens his account with the Boeotarchs divided over whether to offer battle or not. Epaminondas, Malgis and Xenocrates supported engaging the Spartans at once, but Damocleidas, Damophilus and Simangelus were against joining battle. These last three urged that Theban wives and children should be moved to Attica for their safety and that the Thebans should withdraw and prepare for a Spartan siege. The seventh Boeotarch, Brachyllides, was guarding the Cithaeron Pass, and when he returned to the army, sided with Epaminondas, breaking the deadlock. Although these precise details are not recorded elsewhere, they fit easily with the traditions about the omens and debate about fighting. Diodorus is aware of the disagreement between the seven Boeotarchs and even how they disagreed (15.53.3), although he does not provide the detail Pausanias does. The conference and dispute in Pausanias' account is also corroborated in Plutarch, who records (*Pelopidas* 22.1) that while the Boeotian leaders were disputing, Pelopidas was in a state of perplexity.

The additional detail in Pausanias suggests that he might have used a different source to Diodorus, but one which corroborates that part of Diodorus' narrative. Alternatively, if Diodorus was also using Ephorus as a source at this point, did he edit Ephorus more than Pausanias did? Given the other differences in Pausanias' account, the latter seems more likely, but the two accounts in general terms corroborate each other and can be used in conjunction.

This 5th-century BC funerary *stele* of two hoplites, Chairedemos and Lyceas, from Salamania (now in the Piraeus Archaeological Museum, Greece) is useful for the detail of the *sauroter* on both *dory* spears, which the warriors use to hold them while they march, one in the left hand, one in the right. The shield of the left figure is carried by the forearm *porpax* alone, whereas the *antilabe* can be seen on the right figure. (DEA/Archivio J. Lange/Getty Images)

Ruins in the town of Chaeronea, one of which shows an altar with a *tropaion* victory monument with a muscled cuirass and *pteruges*. Kneeling captives are below, while winged victories crown the *tropaion*. Setting up a *tropaion* was the standard signal of a victory, and something the Thebans did after both Tegyra and Leuctra. (DEA/Archivio J. Lange/Getty Images)

Xenophon's account of the pre-battle conference has none of this (*Hellenica* 6.4.6). Xenophon records that the Thebans calculated that if they did not fight, the cities of Boeotia would revolt from them and they would be besieged. Further, if Thebes was cut off from supplies, the city would turn against them. Since several commanders had been exiled before, they decided that it was better to fight than be exiled again. As with so much in Xenophon's account, in isolation it seems reasonable enough. When we consider the factor that Xenophon seems to only record from the Spartan perspective (even though we have seen that he was aware of the Theban omens), his detail on the views of the Theban commanders, not recorded elsewhere, seems suspicious.

In Pausanias' account, once Brachyllides sided with Epaminondas, a unanimous decision was reached to offer battle (9.13.7). Pausanias' next passage seems to be a rationalization of the echelon formation, which was the result of Epaminondas' suspicion of the loyalty of some of the Boeotian contingents, especially the Thespians (9.13.8). He ordered that they could leave camp and head home, which the Thespians and other Boeotians then did.

Pausanias' account then becomes disjointed. He observes that the Spartans and Thebans were both well motivated to fight – the Spartans through experience and the shame of lessening the reputation of Sparta; the Thebans through fighting for their families and country. Next, he jumps forward to when Cleombrotus and other Spartan magistrates have fallen (9.13.10), telling us that the Spartans did not give way despite their distress since it was the greatest dishonour to allow the body of a king to fall into the hands of the enemy. Pausanias then surmises (9.13.11) that the Theban victory at Leuctra was the most famous ever won by Greek over Greek. He gives 47 Boeotian dead (9.13.12) and more than a thousand Spartans.

There is more to consider in Pausanias' account beyond the valuable detail he adds to our knowledge of the battle. The distrust of the Thespians and their departure seems to be introduced in order to explain the numbers of Boeotians present at the battle – the 6,000 Boeotians may equate to the theoretical 7,000 men with seven Boeotarchs less those who departed. This distrust may also be an indication of other divisions within the Boeotian League, and may be seen in the split between the Boeotarchs as to whether to offer battle or not. Polyaenus also refers to this distrust (2.3.3), although he introduces it at a different moment and to explain the echelon tactics. This also tallies with Diodorus and Plutarch; if the Theban allies were of suspect loyalty, Epaminondas could introduce a tactic to keep them out of the fight or minimize their role. They could easily be seen as the 'weaker' units of Diodorus' account. As Diodorus and Plutarch also record, Epaminondas could therefore decide the fight himself with his bravest men and deliver the killing blow to the Spartan right whilst neglecting the rest of the enemy. The idea of disloyal Spartan allies is a factor we will see in Xenophon's account, and may be something which explains Diodorus' crescent attack where the centre of the Spartan forces did not seem to advance.

A funerary *naiskos* (free-standing temple) of Nicomede and her husband, who is clearly a member of the cavalry, dating to the mid-4th century BC. He wears a cloak and tunic, with a sword on his left hip. We rely on Xenophon's account for the actions of the cavalry at Leuctra: they do not feature in any other account, which suggests their actions were entirely within the realms of normal conduct. (Giovanni Dall'Orto via Wikimedia Commons)

The idea of Spartan invincibility was a myth; they had been defeated in battle before, but the perception of many in the ancient world was still that the Spartans were the military force *par excellence*, and, consequently, a reason for their defeat at Leuctra must be sought. The notion that the Spartans were undefeatable increases the drama in our sources' accounts, but it also reflects the status Sparta clearly enjoyed regardless of any reverses suffered before Leuctra. We note this in Xenophon, although, as we shall see, he looks to explain the defeat of Sparta rather than the victory of Thebes. Pausanias' account also contains this, and perhaps Plutarch's idea of the Spartans moving about confusedly falls into this category, too.

More than just an explanation of victory and defeat, however, several of our sources offer explanations of the tactics at Leuctra as they perceived them. Some of these explanations seem either limited or contradictory, but in general they align more often than not. One example is Polyaenus 2.3.3, who records that as Epaminondas led forward the Theban phalanx at Leuctra, the Thespians followed only reluctantly. Epaminondas knew of this, and so said that any Boeotian who wished could leave the ranks. The Thespians withdrew and Epaminondas won a great victory with the remaining formation. This stratagem can be, and has been, read as a contradiction of our other sources, either to be dismissed or used to dismantle another version. As an explanation of Epaminondas' unusual tactic of drawing up the line in echelon, however, it attempts to plausibly explain what happened and seems to combine the idea of drawing up in echelon (and withdrawing from the enemy, found in Diodorus) and also the idea in Pausanias of the Thespians' unreliability. The timing in Polyaenus – that they withdraw as battle was underway – might explain the Boeotian phalanx moving away from the advancing Spartan left wing, whereas in Pausanias their withdrawal seems to be before battle is joined.

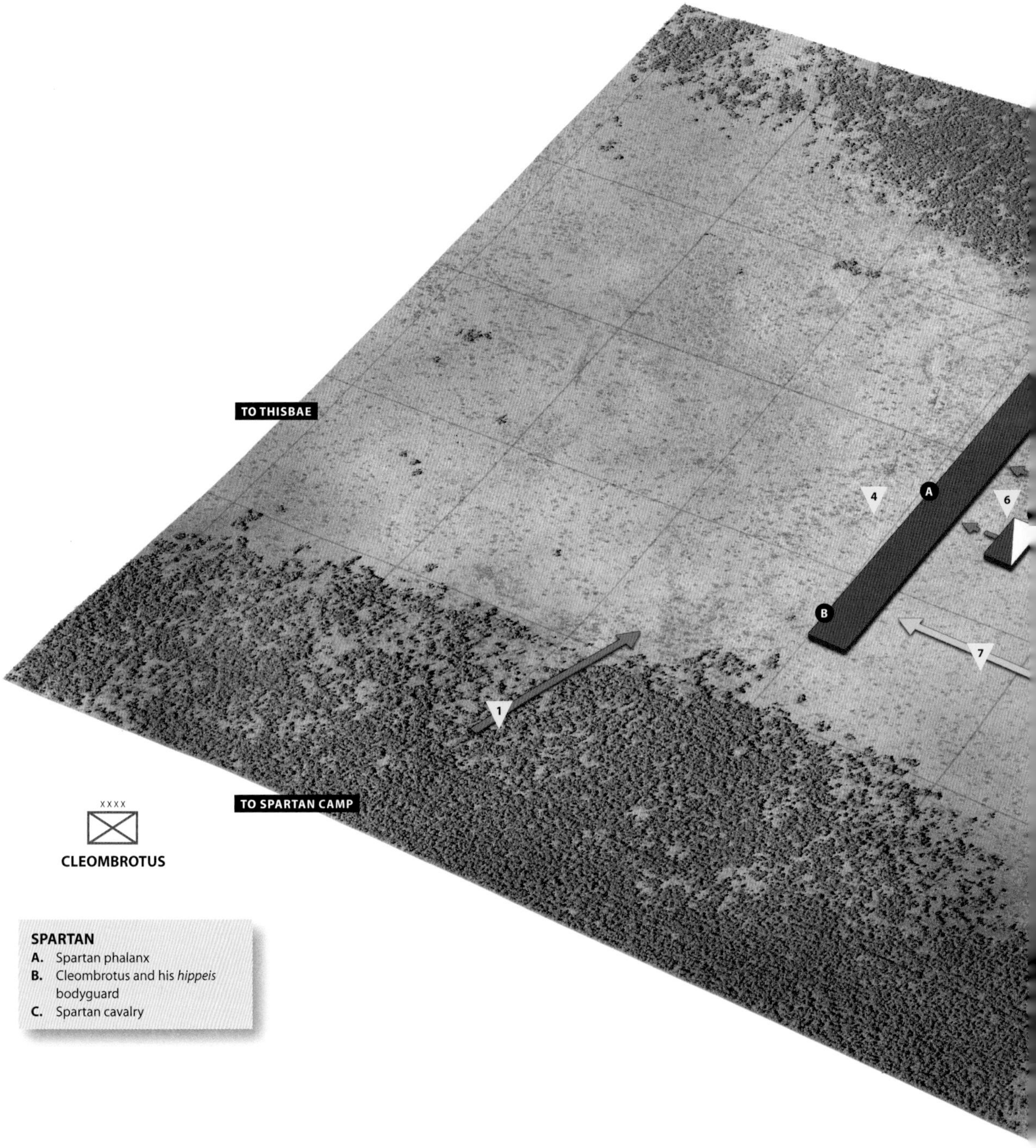

TO THISBAE

4

A

6

B

7

1

xxxx

⊠

CLEOMBROTUS

TO SPARTAN CAMP

**SPARTAN**
**A.** Spartan phalanx
**B.** Cleombrotus and his *hippeis*
    bodyguard
**C.** Spartan cavalry

## EVENTS

**1.** The Spartans descend to the plain from their hillside camp to the west of Leuctra.

**2.** The Thebans move down to the plain from their camp to the north.

**3.** The Theban phalanx is drawn up on the left, up to 50 shields deep according to Xenophon, under Epaminondas. The Sacred Band is also on the left as a front rank of the phalanx, led by Pelopidas. The remainder of the Boeotian phalanx is drawn up in echelon from the Theban contingent. The Theban cavalry, which is only mentioned in one source, is drawn up in front of the phalanx, perhaps as a screen to mask the deployment. The Thebans have only 500 cavalry compared to the Spartans' 1,000 (although the latter is of lesser quality).

**4.** The Spartans draw up their phalanx 12 deep with the Spartans themselves stationed on the right wing, as was customary. Cleombrotus is stationed on the right in the centre of the Spartan contingent surrounded by his *hippeis* bodyguard. The Spartan cavalry are drawn up in front of the formation.

**5.** According to Xenophon (*Hellenica* 6.4.13), the battle begins with a cavalry action. This is entirely absent from other accounts of the battle, which concentrate on the (more important) actions of the victorious Theban left wing. It is entirely possible there was a cavalry action but it was largely inconsequential to the outcome of the battle. Xenophon, however, uses it as an excuse for the (otherwise inexplicable) destruction of the Spartans.

**6.** According to Xenophon, the Spartan cavalry, despite outnumbering the Thebans, is quickly worsted and flees through the centre of the Peloponnesian phalanx (made up of the allies of Sparta), running afoul of the men there.

**7.** It is from Xenophon that we get the detail that the Theban phalanx is 50 shields deep. From our other sources (Diodorus, Plutarch and Pausanias), we find that the dense Theban phalanx on the left charges the Spartan formation on the right, where King Cleombrotus, his bodyguard, and the majority of the Spartans are stationed.

# LEUCTRA, 371 BC: THE OPENING PHASE

Xenophon tells us that the Spartans came to Leuctra from Creusis on the coast to the south-west. The two sides camped on opposing hillsides to the north and south, before meeting in battle on the plain.

TO THESPIAE

TO THEBAN CAMP

TO THEBES

xxxx

EPAMINONDAS

TO EUTRESIS

**THEBAN/BOEOTIAN**
1. Theban phalanx
2. Sacred Band (front rank of the phalanx) under Pelopidas
3. Boeotian phalanx
4. Theban cavalry

TO LEUCTRA

N

Note gridlines are shown at intervals of 250m (273 yards)

If the idea of Epaminondas and Pelopidas comparing notes of massing on the left and attacking the Spartans (and their leadership) directly rings true, then there may be another factor at work here as yet unnoticed. Iphicrates commanded his *peltasts* to withdraw if the Spartan hoplites got too close at Lechaeum (*Hellenica* 4.5.15). Combined with the tactic of the deep Theban phalanx on the left attacking the Spartans, it is not too much of a stretch to see the same withdrawal tactic issued to the remainder of the army. Perhaps Epaminondas (and Pelopidas) had learned the lessons of the history of Spartan weakness. What is more, even in their recent history, events that both Pelopidas and Epaminondas had lived through had reiterated those lessons and provided several examples of Spartan weaknesses. All anyone had to do was pay attention.

As noted earlier, numbers for the two sides at Leuctra differ in our sources, but Pausanias' account seems to be trying to explain why the Theban numbers of 6,000 were smaller than might be expected. Often, Pausanias' mentioning of the hostility of the Spartan allies and their 'reluctance to stand their ground' and 'giving way whenever the enemy attacked them' is taken as a contradiction of Diodorus' account and evidence that the echelon tactics described there either did not exist or did not work. It is interesting that the literary pattern here is one of Theban distrust of their allies, distrust among the Spartan allies and that the Spartans and Thebans themselves 'were not poorly matched adversaries'. It seems as if Pausanias is boiling the battle down to one between Spartans and Thebans. His account of the Spartan allies showing their hostility and giving ground may be read as an explanation of why the army was routed, or why they failed to engage with the forces opposite them in the Theban centre and right wing. It is also possible that

A cavalryman wearing a Boeotian helmet from later in the 4th century BC, on the Alexander Sarcophagus, now in the Istanbul Archaeological Museum. It is probable that the Boeotian cavalry at Leuctra wore the helmet named after their homeland. This cavalryman wears *linothorax* armour and it is likely that Greek cavalry earlier in the century (based on other depictions) were not so heavily armoured, although we do find muscled cuirasses on some. (Marsayas, CC BY-SA 3.0)

## OTHER SOURCE MATERIALS

The brief lives of both Epaminondas and Pelopidas survive in Cornelius Nepos. Despite this, there is little in them on the Battle of Leuctra. Nepos tells us (16.4.2) that Epaminondas was commander-in-chief (*imperator* in the Latin) and that Pelopidas commanded the select corps that first broke the Spartan phalanx. In his life of Epaminondas (15.10.1–2), Nepos records Pelopidas' criticism of Epaminondas for never taking a wife. Epaminondas' response was that he did not lack offspring: he left behind a daughter, the Battle of Leuctra, which was certain to be immortal.

An inscription from Thebes survives, presumably a grave marker, which would seem to suggest that there were others who wished to share in the glory of the victory at Leuctra (Rhodes and Osborne 2003, pp. 150–51). The inscribed epigram records the name of three Thebans – Xenocrates, Theopompus and Mnasilaus – who did not fear 'the host from the Eurotas or the Spartan shield'. 'Thebans are superior in war', proclaims the trophy, 'won through victory by the spear at Leuctra'. The final line of text 'nor did we run second to Epaminondas' has been interpreted as a veiled protest against the (undue) glorification of Epaminondas. There is no need to see implicit criticism in the epigram. It could mean these three performed as well as Epaminondas, and are adding to the glory of their grave marker by including Epaminondas' name. It may also simply mean that they literally ran with Epaminondas – akin to the playwright Aeschylus' epitaph (Athenaeus *Deipnosophistae* 14.627c–d) which recorded that he ran at Marathon.

Certainly, there can be no case to give credit to these three Thebans for the victory rather than or instead of Epaminondas and Pelopidas. Xenocrates matches one of the Boeotarchs named by Pausanias, although we do not know if this was the same individual. This seems unlikely, although the grave marker has been thought to commemorate the leaders who fell at Leuctra (in which case we need to postulate roles for Theopompus and Mnasilaus). Theopompus was the name of one of the exiles who returned to seize Thebes in 379–378 BC (Plutarch *Pelopidas* 8.2) and this might be the same man who would have claim to be equal to Epaminondas. Nonetheless, if Pausanias' low casualty count of 47 is correct then these three, if they died at the battle, would have been honoured highly. Indeed, they would have been honoured even if Diodorus' number of 300 Theban dead is closer to reality.

the Spartan allies giving way refers to when the Thebans presumably 'rolled up' the Peloponnesian line after the Spartans began to flee from the field. The idea of the Thebans knowing what was at stake – country, wives and children – might give some weight to an anecdote in Frontinus (1.11.6): the latter (the only source to do so) records that as the Thebans were about to engage at Leuctra, Epaminondas announced that the Spartans had decreed a massacre of all Theban males and the enslavement of their wives and children, and the razing of Thebes. Polyaenus (2.3.3) records Epaminondas exhorting the phalanx as it advanced, asking them to give him one step and they would achieve victory, matching Diodorus' similar statement (15.56.2).

Diodorus' mentioning of the Spartans advancing in a crescent can also be regarded as problematic, evidence that he (or his source) may be unreliable. At Leuctra, if we combine the idea of Thebans versus Spartans and the reluctance of the Spartan allies in Pausanias' account, then the crescent shape can be better understood; as the two Spartan wings advanced, their reluctant allies in the centre held back, thus creating a concave form. If we combine that with the echelon tactics of Epaminondas (however they might be explained), then the centre and left of the Spartan line could not engage with the Theban phalanx for fear of becoming detached from the (engaged) Spartan right wing. This also ties in with Plutarch's account of Epaminondas threatening to separate the Spartan right from the rest of the Peloponnesian line.

# XENOPHON

And so we come to Xenophon's account of the Battle of Leuctra in his *Hellenica* (6.4.6–15). It is the longest account, is full of detail not found elsewhere and sometimes subverts what we know from our other sources. We might consider that Xenophon deliberately invents a different version

The polymath Xenophon of Athens is one of the most remarkable figures of ancient historiography. His *Hellenica* gives us a continuous history of the Greek world from 411 until 362 BC. For the most part, Xenophon comes across as balanced and reliable, but his material on Thebes is problematic to say the least. Xenophon is guilty of extreme bias against Thebes in favour of Sparta, and this throws his entire account of Leuctra into question. This bust of Xenophon is now in the Aphrodisias Museum, Turkey. (Jona Lendering, CC0 1.0)

of events, but at the same time, he is also persuasive, and his account seems reasonable and balanced. We must remain wary, however, and keep in mind that the other accounts are mostly reconcilable with one another despite one or two caveats.

After his report on the Theban council and omens (see earlier), Xenophon tells us (6.4.8) that Cleombrotus held his final meeting after the morning meal. As was customary, the Spartans drank a little wine with their meal, helping to excite the men for what was to come – a note that will become important for Xenophon's explanation of the defeat.

As both the Spartans and Thebans began arming themselves, Xenophon observes (6.4.9) that those who provided the market and the baggage handlers, along with those who did not wish to fight, withdrew from the Boeotian army. We next find a detail not preserved anywhere else: the Spartan mercenaries commanded by Heiron, the Phocian *peltasts* and the cavalry of the Heracleots and Philiasians are ordered around to cut these Boeotians off and chase them back to the Boeotian camp. If these were the Thespians of other accounts, then their retreat would have been to the north-west, back towards Thespiae itself. This action would seem to be Xenophon's explanation that the ranks of the Boeotians were thereby swelled, and that they became more densely massed, rather than an explanation of the echelon formation (which Xenophon does not mention). At first glance it looks like a corroboration of Plutarch's account of men leaving the Boeotian army, although their return and the reasons given differ. What is more, the idea of reluctant troops, camp followers and baggage handlers adding weight to the phalanx is peculiar. Usually, such men would operate as *psiloi*, light-armed and unarmoured troops who would fight with whatever came to hand, even down to hurling stones. Such troops are usually absent from battle accounts, but are certainly not considered to have added ranks to the phalanx. What is more, adding reluctant troops to a phalanx would be counter-productive. It is entirely possible that the actions of Heiron and the light-armed troops did take place, but were considered to have had no bearing on the outcome of the battle by our other sources. The returning camp followers and baggage handlers is also a way for Xenophon to explain the depth of the Theban phalanx and so make sense of how it defeated the Spartans. It is, however, the first of Xenophon's attempts to distract from the defeat (and its magnitude), and many of Xenophon's details serve to obfuscate what may really have been happening.

Most modern reconstructions of the battle, even when they point out Xenophon's biases, do indeed incorporate his details – the depth of 50 shields or the cavalry engagement, for instance. Some even see the cavalry action, and the Theban combination of infantry and cavalry tactics as described by Xenophon, as the real tactical innovation of the battle (see below). As we have already noted, a deep Theban phalanx goes back, at least, to the Battle of Delium in 424 BC where they were packed 25 deep (Thucydides 4.93.4). Is there a strict need to accept Xenophon's figure of a 50-deep phalanx?

We have a dense column in Diodorus, although no precise depth is given, as well as other suggestions of greater depth to the Theban formation – but only Xenophon provides an actual depth. Whatever qualities Xenophon possesses as a historian are surely abrogated by the faults he so obviously displays against the Thebans, Epaminondas and Pelopidas, as well as his shielding the Spartans (and others) from blame. The attack on the baggage train is seemingly introduced to explain the denseness of the Theban formation – making it an accidental occurrence rather than a deliberate strategy undertaken by Epaminondas. The additional numbers also seem to be introduced to mitigate the Spartan loss to a numerically inferior force. Given the relatively small numbers of the Theban forces, even the addition of the baggage-handlers would surely not have added greatly to their fighting effectiveness. We must also ask how motivated they would have been to participate in the fight. They fled back to the Boeotian lines to seek refuge, not to fight, and they were either non-combatants or men who were, at best, reluctant to fight and who chose to abandon the field. What is more, surely our other accounts of the battle would have made something of the fact that those who chose to leave the Theban ranks were attacked; but they remain silent. Nonetheless, Xenophon's account does in part corroborate that some were reluctant to fight (perhaps the troops of one of the Boeotarchs opposed to fighting), or left, or attempted to leave the Theban ranks.

Xenophon continues (6.4.10) that, since the battlefield was a plain, the Spartans placed their cavalry in front of the phalanx and the Thebans posted their cavalry opposite the Spartan cavalry. The Theban cavalry were well trained, whereas the quality of the Spartan cavalry was poor – and Xenophon was a good judge of cavalry. He blames this on the fact that the Spartans were the least ambitious and the least conditioned physically (6.4.11), whereas the Thebans had recently fought with Orchomenus and Thespiae.

Diodorus (and Ephorus), Plutarch, Pausanias and the anecdotal sources fail to mention the use of cavalry at all at Leuctra. It has been suggested that Xenophon's description reveals a tactical innovation, one which pre-empted the combined infantry and cavalry tactics of Alexander. No ancient

This 5th- or 4th-century BC grave stele from Aigai, Macedonia (modern Vergina, northern Greece), now in the Salonika Archaeological Museum, shows a cavalryman. We can tell this by his *petasos* hat and the fact he carries two javelins. He also wears a *chiton* tunic and *chlamys* cloak, and has a typical *xiphos* sword at his side. Greek cavalry were used for missile harassment, scouting and chasing fleeing enemies; occasionally, they skirmished with other cavalry. (DEA/G. DAGLI ORTI/ DeAgostini/Getty Images)

A fragment of Xenophon's *Hellenica* on papyrus from Oxyrhynchus in Egypt (PSI X 1197 now in the Laurentian Library, Florence). Ironically, it was the discovery of the papyrus remains at Oxyrhynchus in 1900, and especially of the anonymous Oxyrhynchus historian, which led to the realization that Xenophon's version of events is often untrustworthy and that Diodorus of Siculus' version (long berated as inferior) may reflect a more accurate picture in many cases. (Sailko, CC BY 3.0)

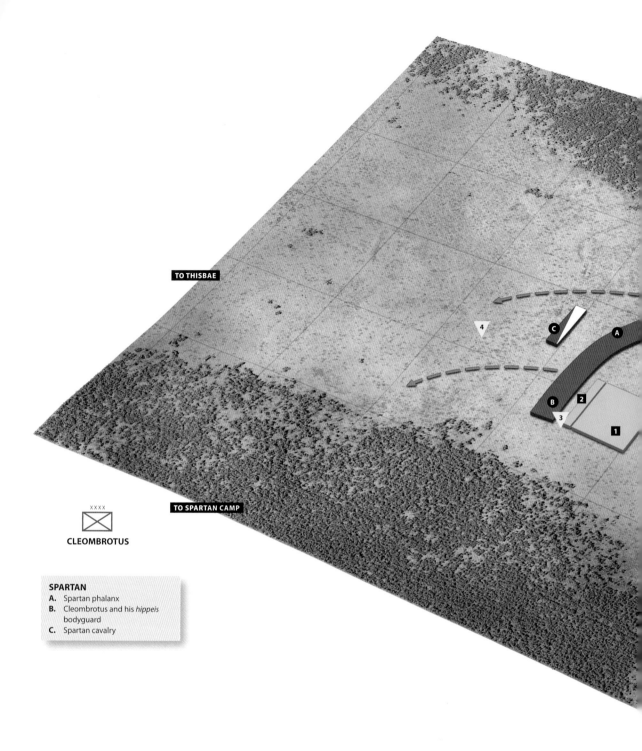

TO THISBAE

TO SPARTAN CAMP

C

A

B

2

3

1

4

XXXX

**CLEOMBROTUS**

**SPARTAN**
**A.** Spartan phalanx
**B.** Cleombrotus and his *hippeis* bodyguard
**C.** Spartan cavalry

## EVENTS

**1.** Diodorus tells us both sides advanced to meet each other. The remainder of the Boeotian phalanx, drawn up in echelon away from the Theban left flank, is instructed not to advance, and even withdraw as the Thebans advance. This tactic means that the remainder of the Spartan forces cannot reach the remainder of the Boeotian army without risking a break in their own phalanx.

**2.** According to Diodorus, the Spartans on the left flank, led by Archidamus (the son of King Agesilaus), do advance, creating a crescent, but they are unable to reach the remainder of the Boeotian forces.

**3.** On the Theban left, the deep phalanx led by the Sacred Band manages to kill Cleombrotus, who is stationed in the front centre of the Spartan right flank. The site of Cleombrotus' death may correspond to the location of the Tropaion monument. The Thebans then break through the Spartan contingent before turning to their right and rolling up the Peloponnesian line.

**4.** The Spartans break and flee back to their camp, followed by the remainder of the Peloponnesians. Xenophon's contention that the Spartans consider offering battle again once they have reached their camp should not be entertained.

# LEUCTRA 371 BC: THE CLOSING PHASES

The advance of the dense Theban phalanx on the left, led by the Sacred Band, results in the death of the Spartan king Cleombrotus, and the rout of Spartan forces.

TO THESPIAE

TO THEBAN CAMP

TO THEBES

xxxx

EPAMINONDAS

TO EUTRESIS

TO LEUCTRA

**THEBAN/BOEOTIAN**
1. Theban phalanx
2. Sacred Band (front rank of the phalanx) under Pelopidas
3. Boeotian phalanx
4. Theban cavalry

N

Note gridlines are shown at intervals of 250m (273 yards)

A cavalry frieze of Greek (mercenary) cavalry from the Tomb of Pericles now in the Antalya Archaeological Museum, Turkey. Xenophon has the cavalry play an important part in the Battle of Leuctra, which no other source records (even though they tell us cavalry was present). Here we see a mixture of Greek headgear – *pilos*, Illyrian and Phrygian helmets, and *petasos* hats. (Ad Meskens/Wikimedia Commons, CC BY-SA 3.0)

author recognized this. In Xenophon, the cavalry action seems to be another explanation of the Spartan loss and introduced to lessen the responsibility for the Theban victory. It is also a distraction for the main charge of the Theban phalanx on the left. Xenophon also seems to make a great deal of what must have been normal practice for cavalry across all Greek armies – training and practice would have been expected of them because they were horsemen. As to being the least strong and least ambitious, these also seem to be unlikely criticisms even in a society that favoured the heavy hoplite above all. This aspect of Xenophon's account may therefore have resulted in an entirely unnecessary distraction for modern scholars. There seems nothing unusual in both sides drawing up their cavalry in front of their phalanxes. Likewise, there is nothing unusual in our accounts of ancient battles to exclude any cavalry action. A cavalry phase, or descriptions of cavalry activity, are often missing from our surviving literary accounts of hoplite battles even when we know cavalry were involved (most famously at Marathon, Herodotus 6.102–117). Cavalry were not considered the important part of a hoplite battle, nor where battles were won and lost; victory was won or lost in the phalanx. Similarly, our accounts usually exclude the actions of light-armed troops. When cavalry and light-armed actions are noteworthy, our accounts do mention them (such as at Sphacteria in 425 BC, Thucydides 4.32–36), otherwise they seem to be considered a normal but un-noteworthy part of battle. We should therefore consider Xenophon's descriptions of light-armed troops and cavalry actions in this vein (even though Xenophon does not).

Xenophon was also more concerned with cavalry and horses than most authors – his son Gryllus joined in the Athenian cavalry and Xenophon wrote (after 371 BC) both *On Horsemanship* and *The Cavalry Commander*. It is possible that nothing significant occurred for the outcome of the Battle of Leuctra in the cavalry engagement. Returning to Polybius' assertion that the battle was a simple affair, Polybius would surely have pointed out the fact that Ephorus had omitted a vital aspect of the battle. As we have seen, Polybius certainly knew of Xenophon's writings, yet in the context of the Battle of Leuctra no mention of him is made. It is entirely possible that too much has been read into the cavalry action as described by Xenophon.

Another line of eight hoplites (in various versions of armour) from the Nereid Monument from Xanthos, Turkey. A depth of eight was one of the standard depths of the classical hoplite phalanx, although at Leuctra we are told by Xenophon that the Spartans adopted a depth of 12 ranks and the Thebans the almost unprecedented depth of 50. The depth of the Theban phalanx would lead to a rethinking of Greek tactics. (Universal History Archive/ Universal Images Group via Getty Images)

Even with these caveats in mind, the next section of Xenophon's account (6.4.12) adds more detail to our picture. Xenophon introduces the Spartan infantry and tells us that each *enomotia* was three files abreast and the phalanx was not more than 12 men deep. This suggests an *enomotia* strength of 36 men. The Thebans opposite them, however, were massed no fewer than 50 shields deep, and this was devised to conquer that part of the Spartan army around the king: if this was defeated, the rest would be easy to overcome. This last observation suggests that Xenophon at least knew of the Theban plan of battle, but he puts it down to chance rather than a deliberate tactic (and he certainly does not mention Epaminondas' part in devising it).

There was nothing new in targeting the commander of an enemy army, and given the Theban massing on their left flank and the position of Cleombrotus on the Spartan right, this is what would have necessarily occurred (and what Pelopidas had achieved at Tegyra). The deliberateness of the dense Theban phalanx, even if it was not 50 ranks deep, still makes Epaminondas' tactics in the battle predetermined, and not random as Xenophon seems to want to make them. The description of the Spartan formation also seems to be used to explain the Spartan defeat – they were only 12 ranks deep and facing (according to Xenophon) one at least 50 ranks deep.

A highly decorative Chalcidian helmet from the mid-4th century BC (note the hinged cheek pieces). It would seem that all helmet designs remained in use in the 4th century BC, with the Boeotian becoming more popular, but 'old-fashioned' styles like the Corinthian remaining common. It is worth remembering that a bronze helmet would remain effective for decades, or longer. (Photo by VCG Wilson/Corbis via Getty Images)

Xenophon might also introduce this detail of the Spartan line depth to explain that the Spartans did nothing on their right flank to counter the depth of the Theban phalanx. The usual depth of the Spartan phalanx was eight ranks, such as at Mantinea in 418 BC (Thucydides 5.68.3), and so the greater depth at Leuctra might be explained as a tactic to counter the depth of the Theban phalanx (it might be the manoeuvre of Plutarch). This, in part, ties in with Plutarch's account, although nothing was achieved before the Theban onrush arrived. The question arises if the Spartans even knew the Thebans themselves opposed them, and the depth of the Theban formation. Since the armies were drawn up on the plain, there was no real way of telling the depth of the enemy lines. Perhaps the cavalry drawn up in front of the phalanxes was used to mask the depth of the Theban formation and the echelon formation of the remainder of the phalanx. If the Spartans did not know the details of the Theban battle plan, then it makes Epaminondas' tactics all the more deliberate (and impressive).

The restored Theban victory monument (Tropaion) at Leuctra. It is most likely that this was erected at the point where the Thebans smashed the Spartan line, perhaps therefore, where Cleombrotus was stationed on the Spartan right, and where he fell. The Thebans therefore probably came from the right of this photo and the Spartan forces stretched away from the viewer. (George E. Koronaios, CC0 1.0)

How drastically does it affect our understanding of the Battle of Leuctra if the Theban phalanx was not 50 ranks deep? We know that a deep phalanx had already been developed and used effectively at Thebes since the late 5th century BC. If the Theban phalanx were only 25 ranks deep, as it had been at Delium, it would still qualify as a deep and dense phalanx (as Diodorus describes) and it would still have been double the depth of the Spartan line. What is more, it was fronted by the Sacred Band, an elite who had defeated the Spartans at Tegyra, were superior in training and were high in confidence. The Theban position on the field could still achieve their goal of defeating the Spartan right – but at relative rank depth of only 2:1, not 4:1. A smaller Theban depth may also explain the Spartan ability to resist the Theban advance for a time – conceivable at 2:1, but much less so at 4:1. The fight over the body of Cleombrotus is also conceivable at odds of 2:1 in that part of the line, but much less explicable if the weight of Theban numbers was much greater. If we accept that the '50 shields deep' included ineffectual men, we must ask what was the combat effective depth of Epaminondas' Theban formation. Twenty-five shields deep worked spectacularly at Delium, and so perhaps a similar depth was used at Leuctra, something that Xenophon's account has possibly obscured.

Xenophon has nothing of the oblique order of the Theban line in his account. He also says nothing specific about the placement of the Thebans on the left. Given his description of the routed baggage-handlers joining the Theban phalanx, is he implying that such a horde made the entire Theban phalanx 50 ranks deep? If we consider for a moment that Xenophon gives the Spartan perspective of the battle, it is possible that an oblique formation was masked from the Spartans by a cavalry screen (the view of Köchly and Rüstow 1852, pp. 171–82), but since Xenophon clearly shows knowledge of the events surrounding the battle, he must have learned of the Theban tactics but chose to remain silent on these. One thing to note on the potential use of cavalry as a screen helps explain a comment in Diodorus (15.53.2) which claims that as the Boeotians advanced, they suddenly caught sight of the Spartan army covering the entire plain of Leuctra and were surprised by its size. This only makes sense if the Spartan cavalry screened the Spartan deployment somewhat, otherwise, the Boeotians will have seen the Spartan phalanx well before it advanced. At the same time, if the Spartan ranks were 12 deep to counter the deep Theban phalanx, they must have seen it before fully deploying.

Xenophon's intention was to explain the Spartan loss, not give credit to Epaminondas or the Thebans for the Theban victory. Xenophon's next statements seem to bear this out when he records (6.4.13) that Cleombrotus began to lead his army against the enemy (this, at least, conforms with Diodorus' picture of both armies charging). Before that, however, the Spartan cavalry had already joined battle with their Theban opposition. The Spartan cavalry had quickly been worsted and had fled straight back into the ranks of their own hoplites, falling foul of them. During their retreat they were attacked by the Theban cavalry. This action, although absent from other accounts, does give an explanation of why the centre of the Peloponnesian formation did not move forward

(explaining Diodorus' crescent where each wing advanced but the centre did not). Other explanations (that the Peloponnesian allies were disloyal) have been offered and those accounts do not mention the cavalry action; it may have been considered insignificant in the outcome of the battle, but it does offer an explanation of the stalled Peloponnesian centre.

Xenophon continues (6.4.13) that on the right Cleombrotus was at first victorious. Xenophon's justification of this is that his body would not have been able to be carried off the field unless the men in front of him held the advantage at the time. This does seem to suggest another excuse from Xenophon, but also that the *othismos* (push) of hoplite battle was actually an undulating to and fro. There could have been moments where the Spartans held ground and even pushed back against the Theban phalanx, even one as deep as 50 shields (although, again, that to-ing and fro-ing is more explicable if the effective Theban phalanx was not as deep as this).

In our other accounts it is Cleombrotus alone, and his death, which is important. Pausanias briefly mentions Cleonymus and other magistrates, but Xenophon goes into much greater depth (6.4.14). He tells us that killed alongside Cleombrotus were Deinon (the polemarch), Sphodrias (one of the king's ten companions) and Cleonymus (Sphodrias' son). Among the other dead were the *hippeis* (the only time Xenophon uses the term), which are also given their alternative title of aides-of-the-polemarch. When these fell, the Spartans withdrew. On the Spartan left wing, when they saw that the right was giving way, they also gave way. Xenophon omits further details. He states that, although defeated, and despite many casualties, the Spartans made their way back to their camp on the slope of a hill. Xenophon offers that the defeated Spartans then thought to fight on and prevent the Thebans from raising a victory trophy. This seems highly unlikely, and is perhaps included to attempt to preserve

The 4th-century BC Thebans took their associations with Heracles very seriously, not only in their adoption of his club as the symbol on their shields but in several other aspects of their society, including the shrine to Iolaus, possibly their interest in wrestling and the association with the (Nemean) lion. (DEA/G. DAGLI ORTI/DeAgostini/ Getty Images)

**THE DEATH OF KING CLEOMBROTUS AT THE BATTLE OF LEUCTRA, 6 JULY 371 BC (PP. 82–83)**

Fierce fighting around King Cleombrotus (**1**) involves the leading men of the Theban Phalanx, the Sacred Band (**2**), taking on the *hippeis* bodyguard (**3**) of the Spartan kings, both elites numbering 300 men and selected from the bravest warriors of each city. At Sparta, there was fierce competition to become a member of the *hippeis*, the succesful candidates often being victors in the Crown Games. The Spartans are 12 ranks deep (and so the *hippeis* are 25 shields wide). The focus of the fiercest fighting, and with corpses piling up around him, Cleombrotus has not shirked from the fray and has already been wounded several times. But now, he has finally fallen. The men around him, including his tent companions and other officers, determine to fight harder to retrieve his body, not knowing that, without its leader, the fate of the Spartan army has been sealed. One of Cleombrotus' companions, Cleonymus, the son of Sphodrias, will be struck down three times in front of his king before finally being killed; his father will also lie dead beside him. The fighting is intense and hand-to-hand. Spears have broken and men have drawn their swords, and some also wrestle with their opponents, trying to gain the upper hand.

Up to the moment Cleombrotus was felled, the Spartans fought bravely, holding back the oncoming Thebans despite the greater depth of the Theban formation. As news of Cleombrotus' death spread through the Spartan ranks, however, panic followed. The Spartans soon broke and fled back to their camp, located behind them on a small hill. The ensuing disaster would be a mortal blow not only to Spartan manpower, but also to Sparta's reputation. The victorious Thebans would cut down many Spartans as they turned to flee, the Spartan allies abandoning their positions to complete the rout. Sparta, whose vaunted hoplites had reputedly never fled from battle, would never regain the ascendancy over Greece that it enjoyed up to the day of Leuctra.

Two 5th-century BC bronze spearheads from Olympia, Greece. The design of Greek spearheads did not change much through the 4th century BC until the radical reforms wrought by Philip II of Macedon. We learn of the lengthening of the spear under Iphicrates at Athens (Cornelius Nepos 11.1, Diodorus 15.44) but we do not know if such reforms were copied in Thebes. (Universal History Archive/ Universal Images Group via Getty Images)

some sense of Spartan dignity. The remaining Spartan commanders, the polemarchs, saw that 1,000 had been killed, including 400 of the 700 Spartiates (6.4.15). According to Xenophon, the remaining Spartan commanders also saw that the allies had lost the heart to fight (with some pleased at the reversal suffered by the Spartans). The Spartans decided to recover the bodies of the dead under a truce. This the Thebans honoured, and they set up their victory monument.

If Xenophon's use of the cavalry engagement is an exaggeration (or an invention) in order to explain, or avoid explaining, the Theban formation during the battle, it would make Xenophon guilty of much more than omission and subversion. It has been regarded as too great a step to accuse him of inventing events. His account (6.4.18) of Archidamus arriving after the battle (and Jason too at 6.4.20) can perhaps be explained as alternative traditions. Archidamus, however, was the son of Xenophon's hero King Agesilaus II, and Xenophon seems to want to shield him from blame. It would have been Archidamus (as commander of the Spartan left, according to Diodorus) who, with the remaining polemarchs, would have made the decision not to fight on.

A 4th-century BC Athenian grave *stele* depicting a cavalryman riding down an enemy, who, unlike similar depictions, defends himself. The cavalryman wears a muscled cuirass, cloak and *petasos* hat, and the victim holds his *aspis* in defence while his *pilos* helmet and cloak have fallen behind him. (DEA/G. Dagli Orti/Getty Images)

While it is no small step to accuse Xenophon of inventing a version of events to fit his design, he is quite clear that Leuctra was indeed a disaster (repeated in *Agesilaus* 2.23). We might argue that there is no way Xenophon could omit the defeat (as he did with Tegyra), but he seems to have done his best to lessen its importance and its impact, and to remove blame from as many Spartans as possible. He also seems to do his utmost to give no credit to the Thebans or to Epaminondas at all. For him it was a Spartan loss, not a Theban victory.

The Spartan flight back to their camp is brushed over in Xenophon's account, but this was a significant moment in terms of the Spartan code of conduct. What is more, the camp was some distance south-west of the battlefield and so Xenophon's idea of the Spartans rejoining battle as being as simple as setting foot once more on the battlefield would not have been an easy thing to do. The Spartans at Leuctra had done exactly what Tyrtaeus (fr. 11, 12) had told them would bring shame on their city – to flee and

A selection of helmets on display at Olympia in the Peloponnese. As can easily be appreciated here, no two helmets were exactly alike, and designs varied widely even within the same type. Often the crests leave no trace, and nor does the furniture which attached the crest to the central ridge of the helmet. (Photo by Toni Salama/Chicago Tribune/Tribune News Service via Getty Images)

The grave *stele* of Stephanos from the first quarter of the 4th century BC, now in the Archaeological Museum of Athens (Inv. 2578). From Tanagra, in Boeotia, we see Stephanos with a *chlamys* cloak and his dog, as well as a *strigil* and oil *aryballos*. When the graves of the Sacred Band were excavated, they were accompanied by *strigils*. The association with wrestling may have links to the Sacred Band and Epaminondas himself (Plutarch *Table Talk* 2.5, Philopoemen 3.2, Polyaenus 2.3.6 and Nepos 15.2.4–5). (Jebulon, CC0 1.0)

not stand firm. Even though Xenophon tries to argue that the Spartans were in favour of renewing the battle, the damage had already been done to both manpower and reputation.

Xenophon must have known that all of Greece praised Epaminondas for 'his' victory at Leuctra soon after the battle, and yet he does not try to counter those claims explicitly and instead offers a version of what 'really' happened. Blame in Xenophon lies especially with the death of Cleombrotus and the poor quality of the Spartan cavalry. The lessened impact of the battle can be seen in Xenophon's version with the Spartans willing to keep fighting but being prevented from doing so by the number of Spartan dead and the allies' unwillingness to continue. Unfortunately, the situation is complicated further by Xenophon's eventual mentioning of Pelopidas and Epaminondas later in his narrative and even the arguably positive way he treats them there (Pelopidas in *Hellenica* 7.1.33–38, Epaminondas in *Hellenica* 7.4.13 and *Hellenica* 7.4.40–5.25). If we are brave enough to level the accusation of invention at Xenophon and largely reject his version of events for the Battle of Leuctra, however, it actually makes our picture of the battle remarkably clear since on the whole our other sources, small and large, paint the same picture and several complications are removed.

In all of the accounts preceding Xenophon's in this analysis, the role of Epaminondas and Pelopidas are paramount. Xenophon's exclusion of them from his account appears to be inexcusable. We should bear in mind his omission of aspects such as Archidamus' absence and Jason of Pherae's arrival after it. Xenophon seeks to remove any stain from his hero Agesilaus' son by having him take no part in the battle. Thus, Archidamus probably was present at Leuctra (and most likely on the left wing) and should share in the ignominy of that defeat, even of being paramount in accepting the loss, irrespective of the shielding Xenophon would offer him. Anderson's observations that Xenophon writes from the Spartan perspective and from notes are unsatisfactory (Anderson 1970, p. 199). Nor is the fact that Xenophon was a contemporary of the battle an excuse for his errors. Both Anderson and Hanson accept the argument that Xenophon did not appreciate either the magnitude of what had happened at Leuctra or Epaminondas' tactics. However, Xenophon lived through the entirety of the Theban hegemony over Greece and knew first-hand how important Leuctra was, and how widely Epaminondas was praised for the victory. Moreover, several of the reasons Xenophon gives for the Spartan defeat – heavy drinking (*Hellenica* 6.4.8), poor morale (ibid. 6.4.2–6) and the worthless cavalry (ibid. 6.4.10–11) – are hard to explain in a Spartan army.

## A SUMMARY OF THE SOURCES

Hanson rejects Diodorus and Plutarch (who wrote 'hundreds of years' later) and prefers the contemporary Xenophon for his more basic, but clear explanations of the events of the battle (1988, p. 206). Hanson also points out that Xenophon's account is the earliest and the only one by an experienced military man. We should recall, however, that Diodorus, Plutarch (and Pausanias) used sources composed closer to the date of the events and none of those accounts aligns closely with Xenophon's version. The evidence of the legacy of Leuctra in authors such as Polyaenus, Frontinus, Nepos and others also do not resemble Xenophon's version but largely concur with that given by Diodorus and Plutarch. Usually it is in minutiae that our sources disagree; but choosing to follow the single narrative of Xenophon is in my view radical and wrongheaded. Xenophon may well be more reasonable and more balanced as a writer for many events of the 4th century BC, but that does not make his account of Leuctra correct. The *Hellenica Oxyrhynchia* also agrees more often with Diodorus than with Xenophon's version of events. No other writer mentions Xenophon's picture of the battle even when they refer to Xenophon and his writings elsewhere. Xenophon's account does indeed make sense as an account of a battle, but it does not seem to be the Leuctra other sources were writing about, and nor is it the simple affair of Polybius. Nonetheless, it is possible to use some of Xenophon's details, provided they can be incorporated into the narrative of the battle presented by our other sources. However, simply because Xenophon includes it does not necessarily mean it needs to be incorporated into our overall picture of the battle.

When we examine the anecdotal accounts of Leuctra, it is, as far as we are able to tell, the picture from Diodorus, Plutarch and Pausanias that they overwhelmingly support, not that in Xenophon. They all name Epaminondas and Pelopidas, which immediately places them outside what we might call the Xenophontic tradition. What is more, as we know, many of the anecdotes are also independent of the historical records as we have them and so represent either separate historical traditions or more detailed ones that our longer sources do not record. Given the differences in some details, the former possibility of separate traditions is far more likely. In summary, whenever Xenophon offers details from the Spartan perspective which do not contradict what we know, we should consider using Xenophon's details; but when Xenophon can be contradicted by the weightier historical tradition, then we are at liberty to side with that tradition, regardless of the merits of Xenophon as a writer, historian or indeed general.

A 5th or 4th century polychrome terracotta Boeotian shepherd, perhaps a *kriophoros* 'ram bearer', from Tanagra (now in the Archaeological Museum of Athens). The tunic, *chlamys* cloak and *pileus* hat were all retained or, in the case of helmets, modelled on existing forms. The tanned skin evident in the paint colour is a reminder of the hardy lifestyles of all Greek warriors. (Giovanni Dall'Orto via Wikimedia Commons)

# AFTERMATH

## CASUALTIES

A further aspect of the Battle of Leuctra, and one that ties in with the troublesome numbers of soldiers engaged explored earlier in this work, are the casualty figures. Pausanias gives only 47 Boeotian dead (9.13.12) and more than 1,000 Lacedaemonians; Diodorus has 4,000 Peloponnesian dead and 300 Boeotians (15.56.4). Xenophon records almost 1,000 Lacedaemonian dead and 400 of the 700 Spartiates present (6.4.15). Xenophon gives no number for the Boeotian casualties. There seems to be some agreement in the 1,000 dead of Pausanias and Xenophon. Plutarch records a similar figure to Pausanias, as does Xenophon, although not in his account of the battle itself: in *Sayings of Kings and Commanders* 12 (*Moralia* 193B), he states there were more than 1,000 Spartan dead, and in his *Agesilaus* (28.5) records that 1,000 Lacedaemonians fell. These discrepancies in the numbers are impossible to reconcile.

Five types of helmet (a Boeotian and Attic example are missing), all of which were in use in the early 4th century BC. Top row (left to right): Illyrian, Corinthian. Bottom row: Phrygian, *pilos*, Chalcidian. The *pilos* helmet here is much more decorated than standard examples. (MisterPlus65, CC BY-SA 4.0)

Even if we accept Xenophon's low number of only 700 Spartiate citizens at the battle, the loss of 400 of them represented 60 per cent casualties, and a reduction to her citizen body that, as history had shown, was nigh-on impossible for Sparta to replace. Spartan armies henceforth would need to rely more and more on allies and mercenaries. Sparta had lost her king, several of her commanders and the entirety of her best warriors who fought in the *hippeis*. The higher casualty estimates give immense losses; the 4,000 casualties of Diodorus represent 40 per cent of the entire Peloponnesian force. Diodorus later (15.63.1) says that Sparta had cast away many of her young men at Leuctra and there was no getting them back. If we accept Pausanias' Theban losses of a mere 47 out of 300 men, for the Spartans to fight on would have meant total destruction.

## THE SHOCKWAVES OF DEFEAT

The immediate aftermath of the Battle of Leuctra was probably one of shock. The mystique of Spartan dominance on the battlefields of Greece, of Spartan superiority in valour and as a fighting force, had been shattered. In one fell swoop, the Spartan hegemony over all of Greece was ended. Unlike at Tegyra in 375 BC, where only a small number of participants saw the men of two Spartan *morai* run, at Leuctra all the Peloponnesian allies witnessed it along with most of the men of the Boeotian League; Sparta's utter defeat was plain for all to see. Pausanias even makes the point of Sparta covering up her disasters (9.13.11–12), which she could not do after Leuctra. Sparta had suffered defeats before, but never one so devastating by an outnumbered force. Sparta had no answer to the Theban tactics devised specifically to counter them. Diodorus talks of the Theban victory as miraculous (15.56.3), where the Thebans had defeated the 'invincible leaders of Greece' (15.56.4).

A much simpler example of a *pilos* helmet, now in the Metropolitan Museum of Art, New York (Inv. 08.258.14). Even with such a simple design, there were wide variations in the shape. The hole may have been for a simple chinstrap, or where it was hung as a votive offering. Over time, such helmets were fitted with cheek pieces and helmet crests. (Metropolitan Museum of Art, CC0 1.0)

Immediately after the battle, Epaminondas kept the Spartans besieged in Leuctra (Pausanias 9.14.1–2), but then allowed them to return home when he learned more Spartans were approaching as a relief force. The defeat also allowed the focus of the war to shift from Boeotia to the Spartan homeland of Laconia in the Peloponnese. Xenophon's aftermath differs from that of Pausanias, however, with preparations for further conflict being made in Sparta (led by Archidamus, who Xenophon claims was not at Leuctra, *Hellenica* 6.4.18) and with loyal allies. Jason of Pherae also arrived after the battle in Xenophon's version (6.4.20–25), and then advised the Thebans not to destroy Sparta.

In 370 BC, Epaminondas invaded the Peloponnese, this time with Pelopidas also as Boeotarch (Plutarch *Pelopidas* 24.1, Diodorus 15.62.4). They found willing allies in the Arcadians and in Argos (Pausanias 9.14.4); Plutarch and Diodorus had Elis, Argos, all Arcadia and most of Laconia detach themselves from the Peloponnesian Confederacy and ally with Thebes and the Boeotians (*Pelopidas* 24.1, Diodorus 15.62.5). Combined, these men placed themselves under Epaminondas' command (recognizing his generalship, Diodorus 15.63.1) and marched on Sparta. They

The 3.8m-tall Lion of Chaeronea marks the burial of 254 skeletons, probably the final resting place of the Sacred Band who were destroyed to a man there in 338 BC by Alexander of Macedon, only 40 years after their re-establishment in c. 378 BC. The Lion, set up by the Thebans, further emphasizes the connection with Heracles, and led to emulations such as the Lion of Amphipolis set up later in the 4th century BC. (DEA/G. Dagli Orti/Getty Images)

crossed the Eurotas River into the Spartan homelands with up to 70,000 men (*Pelopidas* 24.2; Diodorus gives 50,000). This was the first invasion of the Spartan homeland in centuries, but Agesilaus did not come out against them. Instead, Epaminondas freed the Helots and refounded the city of Messene on Mt Ithome in Messenia as a focus of anti-Spartan feeling in the former Helot home territory. The invasion lasted into 369 BC and beyond the allotted term of Epaminondas' and Pelopidas' Boeotarchies. Charges were brought against them at Thebes, but dropped, and Epaminondas was again elected Boeotarch. He promptly moved to invade the Peloponnese once more.

The ensuing Theban hegemony would face struggles against Athens (now allied with Sparta, recognizing the threat of a strengthened Thebes) and other opponents throughout Greece, but the Spartan dominance of Greek politics and warfare of more than a century was broken and could never be restored. The Boeotian phalanx would face the armies of Sparta again at Mantinea in 362 BC; once again, they would be defeated, further eroding the Spartan legacy.

# THE BATTLEFIELDS TODAY

## TEGYRA

The exact location of the Battle of Tegyra is debated. The narrow pass at which the Thebans encountered the Spartans returning from Locris can, however, be one of only a few places. What was Lake Copais are now fields, although it is possible to trace what may have been the shoreline north of Orchomenus in the hills that surround the plain. Modern Orchomenus will allow you to gain views of the entire area, especially from the spectacular acropolis, all the way across the plain of the drained lake to Thebes (modern Thiva). The march of Pelopidas north and east of Orchomenus in 375 BC must have followed this route (in order for his forces to encounter the returning Spartans). The first potential battle site you come to north of Orchomenus is at Polyira. Taking the Epar. Od. Orchomenu–Dionisou road north to Dionisos and then the Eparchikai Comitatus Iter Atalante–Imperat road north out of Dionisos, a right turn towards Kefalovriso will bring you to this site. It had a Mycenean temple, which might accord with the shrine to Apollo of Plutarch's description. It is not necessarily a narrow pass, however.

A frieze of the *Amazonomachy* from the Mausoleum at Halicarnassus (*c.* 353–350 BC), Caria (modern Bodrum, Turkey) now in the British Museum. The depiction of the sword here is particularly illustrative. Despite the vast number of depictions in art, portraiture and funerary reliefs of Corinthian helmets pushed back on the head (as two figures here show), it is still doubted whether this was done in reality. (Ann Ronan Pictures/Print Collector/Getty Images)

Further along the same road, which turns to the east, will bring you to another candidate for the battlesite, Pyrgos. The site of this village requires a slight southwards turn along the former shore of Lake Copais. North of Pyrgos, however, on the road to the modern towns of Loutsi and Kyrtoni, is a narrow pass which might fit the bill of the battle site; this is the one on which we have based our earlier battle reconstruction. The site is also visible from the acropolis of Orchomenus, which was of concern to Pelopidas after his victory.

# LEUCTRA

Returning to Orchomenus from the pass above Pyrgos, you can make your way south-west to Highway 3. Taking this south and then east will bring you to Haliartus (modern Aliartos). There, a turn to the south will take you to Mavrommati and then Thespies (ancient Thespiae) and Leontari. From Thespies, looking south you survey the fields towards Leuctra. By road, you are best to join the Epar. Od. Thivas–Paralia Sarantis road and then branch off on to the Epar. Od. Thespion–Erithron road which will bring you to Ellopia. From there, heading east on the same road (which becomes the Lefktron–Thisvis) will bring you directly to the Leuctra Tropaion, just north-west of the town of Leuctra. The battlefield stretches away from this monument which is close to the hills on the field's south side. In our reconstruction, we have assumed that the Tropaion marked the point where the Theban left clashed with the Spartan right and perhaps the point at which Cleombrotus fell. Our reconstruction therefore considers that if you stand at the Tropaion facing north, the Thebans drew up to your right, the Spartans to your left. Just north of the Tropaion is a modern canal. The battlefield itself consists of private farmland, although there are minor roads which lead on to it. It is clear that this fertile land has remained relatively unchanged since the time of the battle, although, other than the Tropaion, the battle itself will have left little trace. To the south-west of the Tropaion are two hills; the Spartan camp was probably drawn up on the furthest of these. The Theban camp was probably on the low hills north-east of the Tropaion across the battlefield. Several minor roads cross this ground. Other than the collections in the National Archaeological Museum in Athens, there are finds in various museums of the ancient towns of Boeotia, especially the Archaeological Museum of Thebes (which continuing east on the Thespion–Erithron road will bring you to).

This Corinthian helmet, now in the British Museum, shows a clear finishing wound, probably delivered by a *sauroter* once the wearer was felled. Other equipment, and even skulls, reveal similar wounds. Helmets like this were then dedicated at temples and hung up to commemorate the victory. (Universal History Archive/ Universal Images Group via Getty Images)

# BIBLIOGRAPHY

## Classical works

Aeschines (trans. C.D. Adams), Cambridge, MA and London: Harvard University Press (1919)

Aristotle (trans. H. Rackham), 21 vols: Vol. 20: *Athenian Constitution*, and Vol. 21, *Politics*, Cambridge, MA and London: Harvard University Press (1932/1935)

Athenaeus (trans. C.B. Gulick), *The Deipnosophists*, 12 vols: Vol. 6, Books 13 and 14, Cambridge, MA and London: Harvard University Press (1937)

Caesar (trans. A.G. Peskett), *Civil Wars*, Cambridge, MA and London: Harvard University Press (1914)

Cornelius Nepos (trans. J.C. Rolfe), Cambridge, MA and London: Harvard University Press (1929)

Dio Chrysostom (trans. H.L. Crosby), *Discourses: Discourse 45*, Cambridge, MA and London: Harvard University Press (1946)

Diodorus Siculus (trans. C.L. Sherman), 12 vols: Vol. 7, Books XV.20–XVI.65, Cambridge, MA and London: Harvard University Press (1963)

Frontinus (trans. C.E. Bennett), *The Stratagems*, Cambridge, MA and London: Harvard University Press (1925)

Lysias (trans. W.R.M. Lamb), Cambridge, MA and London: Harvard University Press (1930)

*Minor Attic Orators* (trans. K.J. Maidment and J.O. Burtt), 2 vols: Vol. 2, *Dinarchus*, Cambridge, MA and London: Harvard University Press (1941–54)

Pausanias (trans. W.H.S. Jones), *Description of Greece*, 5 vols: Vol. 4, Book 9, Cambridge, MA and London: Harvard University Press (1918–55)

Plato (trans. W.R.M. Lamb), 12 vols: Vol. 3, *Symposium*, Cambridge, MA and London: Harvard University Press (1925)

Plutarch (trans. B. Perrin et al, *Plutarch's Lives*, 11 vols: Vol. 1, *Life of Lycurgus*; Vol. 4, *Life of Lysander*; Vol. 5, *Life of Pelopidas, Life of Agesilaus*; Vol. 7, *Life of Alexander*; Vol. 10, *Life of Philopoemen*, Cambridge, MA and London: Harvard University Press (1914–21)

——, (trans. F.C. Babbitt et al), *Plutarch's Moralia*, 16 vols: Vol. 1, *How a Man May Become Aware of His Progress in Virtue*; Vol. 3, *Sayings of Spartans, Spartan Customs, Sayings of Kings and Commanders*; Vol. 4, *Roman Questions, Were the Athenians More Famous in War or in Wisdom*; Vol. 6, *Concerning Talkativeness*; Vol. 7, *On the Sign of Socrates*; Vol. 8, *Table Talk*; Vol. 9, *The Dialogue on Love*; Vol. 11, *On the Malice of Herodotus*; Vol. 12, *Whether Land or Sea Animals Are Cleverer*; Vol. 14, *That Epicurus Actually Makes a Pleasant Life Impossible*, Cambridge, MA and London: Harvard University Press (1927–67)

Polyaenus (trans. P. Krentz and E.L. Wheeler), *Stratagems of War*, 2 vols, Chicago: Ares Publishers (1994)

Polybius (trans. W.R. Paton), *The Histories*, 6 vols, Cambridge, MA and London: Harvard University Press (1922–26)

Strabo (trans. H.L. Jones), *The Geography*, 8 vols, Cambridge, MA and London: Harvard University Press (1917–32)

Thucydides (trans. C.F. Smith), 4 vols, Cambridge, MA and London: Harvard University Press (1919–23)

Xenophon (trans. C.L. Brownson), *Hellenica*, 2 vols, Cambridge, MA and London: Harvard University Press (1918–21)

——, (trans. E.C. Marchant), *Memorabilia, Oeconomicus, Symposium, and Apology*, Cambridge, MA and London: Harvard University Press (1923)

——, (trans. E.C. Marchant), *Scripta Minora (Spartan Constitution, Cavalry Commander, On Horsemanship)*, Cambridge, MA and London: Harvard University Press (1925)

## Modern works

Anderson, J.K., *Military Theory and Practice in the Age of Xenophon*, Berkeley and Los Angeles: University of California Press (1970)

Bruce, I.A.F., *An Historical Commentary on the 'Hellenica Oxyrhynchia'*, Cambridge: Cambridge University Press (1967)

Buck, R.J., *A History of Boeotia*, Edmonton: University of Alberta Press (1979)

——, *Boiotia and the Boitian League, 432–371 B.C.*, Edmonton: University of Alberta Press (1994)

Buckler, J., *The Theban Hegemony 371–362 BC*, Cambridge, MA and London: Harvard University Press (1980)

Cartledge, P., *The Spartans: An Epic History*, London: Macmillan (2002)

——, *Thermopylae: The Battle that Changed the World*, London: Macmillan (2006)

——, *Thebes: The Forgotten City of Ancient Greece*, New York: Abrams Press (2020)

Cawkwell, G., 'Introduction' to Xenophon, *A History of My Times* (trans. R. Warner), Harmondsworth: Penguin Books (1979)

Delbrück, H., *Geschichte der Kriegskunst 1: Das Altertum*, 2nd Ed. (Berlin, 1908); available in English as *History of the Art of War 1: Antiquity* (trans. Walter Renfroe), Westport, Connecticut: Greenwood Press (1975)

Demand, N.H., *Thebes in the Fifth Century: Hercules Resurgent*, London: Routledge (1982)

DeVoto, J., 'Pelopidas and Kleombrotos at Leuktra', *The Ancient History Bulletin* 3, pp. 115–18 (1989)

——, 'The Theban Sacred Band', *The Ancient World* 23, pp. 3–19 (1992)

——, 'The λοχαγοι of the Theban Sacred Band', *Alpha to Omega: Studies in Honour of George John Szemler on his Sixty-Fifth Birthday* (ed. W.J. Cherf), Chicago: Ares, pp. 59–68 (1993)

Esposito, G., *Armies of Ancient Greece Circa 500 to 338 BC: History, Organization and Equipment*, Barnsley: Pen & Sword Military (2020)

Fields, N., *The Spartan Way*, Barnsley: Pen & Sword Military (2013)

Forrest, W.G., *A History of Sparta 950–192 BC*, London: Hutchison University Library (1968)

Georgiadou, A., *Plutarch's Pelopidas*, Stuttgart and Leipzig: Teubner (1997)

Griess, T.E. (ed.), *Ancient and Medieval Warfare: The West Point Military History Series*, Wayne, New Jersey: Avery Publishing Group (1984)

Hanson, V.D., 'Epameinondas, the Battle of Leuktra (371 B.C.), and the "Revolution" in Greek Battle Tactics', *Classical Antiquity* 7, pp. 190–207 (1988)

Henry, W., *Greek Historical Writings*, Chicago: Argonaut Inc. (1967)

Hodkinson, S. and Powell, A. (eds.), *Sparta & War*, Swansea: The Classical Press of Wales (2006)

Kelly, T., 'Did the Argives Defeat the Spartans at Hysiae in 669 B.C.?', *American Journal of Philology* 91, pp. 31–42 (1970)

——, *A History of Argos to 500 B.C.*, Minneapolis: University of Minnesota Press (1976)

——, 'The Traditional Enmity between Sparta and Argos: The Birth and Development of a Myth', *American Historical Review* 75, pp. 971–1003 (1970)

Köchly, H.A.T. and Rüstow, W., *Geschichte des Griechischen Kriegswesens von der ältesten Zeit bis auf Pyrrhos*, Aarau: Verlags-Comptoirs (1852)

Konijnendijk, R., 'On the dancing floor of Ares: The battle of Leuctra', *Ancient Warfare* 9.2, pp. 26–33 (2013)

Kromayer, J. and Veith, G., *Schlactenatlas zür antiken Kriegesgeschichte*, Parts I–V, Leipzig: H. Wagner and E. Debes (1922–29), available in English as *The Atlas of Ancient Battlefields* (trans. Tristan Skupniewicz), Oświęcim: Napoleon V (2019)

——, *Antike schlactfelder in Griechenland*, 2 vols, Berlin: Weidmann (1903–07)

Larsen, J.A.O., *Greek Federal States*, Oxford: Clarendon Press (1968)

Lazenby, J.F., *The Spartan Army*, Warminster: Aris & Phillips (1985)

Leitao, D., 'The Legend of the Sacred Band', in Nussbaum M.C. and Shivola, J. (eds.), *The Sleep of Reason: Erotic Experience and Sexual Ethics in Ancient Greece and Rome*, Chicago and London: The University of Chicago Press, pp. 143–69 (2002)

Ma, J., 'Chaironeia 338: Topographies of Commemoration', *Journal of Hellenic Studies* 128, pp. 72–91 (2008)

McGing, B., *Polybius' Histories*, Oxford: Oxford University Press (2010)

McKechnie, P.R. and Kern, S.J., *Hellenica Oxyrhynchia*, Warminster: Aris & Phillips (1988)

Rhodes, P.J. and Osborne, R. (eds. and trans.), *Greek Historical Inscriptions 404–323 BC*, Oxford: Oxford University Press (2003)

Rockwell, N., *Thebes: A History*, London and New York: Routledge (2017)

Rusch, S.M., *Sparta at War: Strategy, Tactics, and Campaigns, 550–362 BC*, London: Frontline Books (2011)

Shrimpton, G.S., 'Plutarch's Life of *Epaminondas*', *Pacific Coast Philology* 6, pp. 55–59 (1971)

——, 'The Theban Supremacy in Fourth-Century Literature', *Phoenix* 25, pp. 310–18 (1971)

Snodgrass, A.M., *Arms and Armour of the Greeks*, Ithaca, NY: Cornell University Press (1967)

Tod, M.N., *A Selection of Greek Historical Inscriptions*, 2 vols, Oxford: Clarendon Press (1948)

Tomlinson, R.A., *Argos and the Argolid*, London and Ithaca, NY: Routledge (1972)

Tuplin, C.J., 'The Leuctra Campaign: Some Outstanding Problems', *Klio* 69, pp. 72–107 (1987)

# INDEX